D1304952

FOR MOM

Chicken Rising © D. Boyd, 2019

First Edition

Printed in Quebec by Gauvin

Library and Archives Canada Cataloguing in Publication

Boyd, D. (Dawn), author, illustrator
    Chicken rising / D. Boyd.

ISBN 978-1-77262-034-4 (softcover)

    1. Comics (Graphic works). I. Title.
PN6733.B72C55 2019   741.5'971   C2018-905606-1

Chicken Rising is a graphic memoir and as such there are many brand names and characters which appear throughout the book. These are placed here to represent a verisimilitude of the reality of 1970s popular culture and are in no way claims on copyright, nor intended in a derogatory way. All copyrights are held by the original creators.

Conundrum Press
Wolfville, Nova Scotia, Canada
www.conundrumpress.com

Distributed in Canada by Litdistco. Distributed in the US by Consortium.

Conundrum Press acknowledges the financial support of the Canada Council for the Arts, the Province of Nova Scotia's Creative Industries Fund, and the government of Canada through the Canada Book Fund.

CHICKEN RISING

D. BOYD

PRESCHOOL

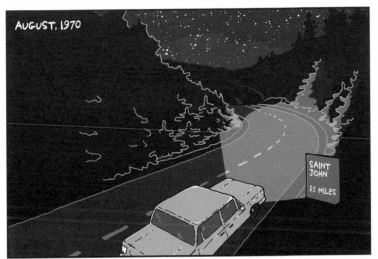

AUGUST, 1970

SAINT JOHN

25 MILES

SO **BOTH** YOUR SISTERS ARE COMING TO WORK WITH US?

YEP. KEEP IT IN THE FAMILY.

WAKE UP, DAWN.

I'M AWAKE.

DO YOU SEE THAT **GLOW**? WE'RE ALMOST THERE.

IS THERE ANY MORE OF THAT **CHICKEN**?

OH, THERE'S GONNA BE A **LOT** MORE WHERE **THAT** CAME FROM!

SEPTEMBER, 1970

I'M AN OLD COWHAND...
FROM THE RIO GRANDE!

THAT CHICKEN SMELLS
SOME JEEZLY GOOD!

WELL, THAT'S
BECAUSE IT IS!

8

LOOKIN' SHIP-SHAPE!

MAKE YOURSELF **USEFUL.** GO GRAB A BOX OF NAPKINS.

SO ARE WE **READY FOR BUSINESS** THERE, GIRLS?

YOU BET, CLINT!

DAMN RIGHT!

ALRIGHT! I'M GONNA OPEN 'ER UP!

COME ON IN, FOLKS! BEST CHICKEN IN TOWN!

WHAT CAN I GETCHA?

9

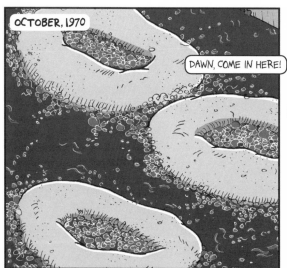

OCTOBER, 1970

DAWN, COME IN HERE!

I'M MAKING **DONUTS**.

YAWN

SEE HOW THEY SINK, THEN COME BACK UP, AND THEN... YOU HAVE TO FLIP THEM.

LIKE THAT.

CAN I HAVE ONE?

NO.

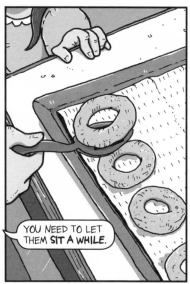

YOU NEED TO LET THEM **SIT A WHILE**.

CAN I DO ONE?

NO. YOU SHOULDN'T EVEN BE AROUND THESE FRYERS.

YAWN

DON'T STEP ON MY CLEAN FLOOR.

STEP ON THE BOXES.

WHAT THE HELL ARE YOU DOING UP THIS LATE ANYWAY?

NOVEMBER, 1970

LOOK AT US. DO DICK AND I LOOK **FUNNY?**

SALLY SAID, 'YOU **DO!** YOU **DO** LOOK FUNNY!'

GOOD, GOOD.

OKAY DEAR, I GUESS THAT'S IT FOR TODAY.

YOUR PARENTS SHOULD BE VERY **PLEASED** WITH YOU.

WAIT! COME **BACK** HERE!

YOU HAVE TO HOLD MY HAND!

I **KNOW** HOW TO CROSS THE STREET. JEEZ.

Fun with Dick and Jane

LOOKIT WHAT I DID TODAY!

SYBIL, SHE JUST RAN OFF AND **CROSSED THE STREET** WITHOUT ME.

I LOOKED BOTH WAYS!

YOU **HAVE** TO DO WHAT MISS RIVERS TELLS YOU.

SEE YOU MONDAY.

GODDAMNED COLD **CHICKEN**. GONNA GIVE ME **ARTHRITIS**.

OKAY, SHOW ME.

YOUR **Q** IS BACKWARDS. SEE, IT LOOKS LIKE A **G**.

DON'T MAKE THAT FACE. YOU HAVE TO LEARN HOW TO TAKE **CRITICISM**.

SHE'S KIND OF AN OLD FUDDY-DUDDY, ISN'T SHE?

I'M ONLY BEING **HARD** ON YOU BECAUSE YOU HAVE TO BE **AHEAD OF THE GAME** BEFORE YOU START **GRADE ONE!**

NOW LET'S HAVE A **POP**.

DECEMBER, 1970

IT'S NOT **FAIR**.

HE JUST WANTS TO **EAT**. HE'S NOT **REALLY** THE **BAD GUY**.

I GUESS YOU GO FOR THE **UNDERDOG**, DEAR.

I SAW 'UNDERDOG' BUT I DON'T LIKE HIM. DOGS ARE **ALWAYS** THE **HEROES**.

HAHA, NO...

THE UNDERDOG ALWAYS GETS THE **SHIT END** OF THE STICK. THE **LOSER**.

SO THEN 'UNDERDOG' ISN'T **REALLY** THE UNDERDOG...

NO, I GUESS NOT.

YOU'RE DOING IT WRONG. FOLD IT UNDER THERE.

THERE'S NO POINT IN DOING SOMETHING IF YOU'RE **NOT** GOING TO DO IT **RIGHT**.

MAY, 1971

IT'S SOME PRETTY, BUT **JEEEZ** YOU'RE GONNA BE AWFULLY FAR FROM **TOWN**!

IT'LL BE A BIT OF AN ADJUSTMENT, RITA.

OH SYB, IT'S **REAL** CUTE. SMELLS SOME NICE, TOO...

EH, MARY ANNE?

YEAH. IT'S RIGHT NICE.

15

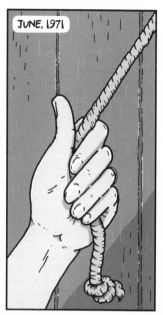

JUNE, 1971

YOU STAY THERE!

WHINE!

THIS WILL BE **YOUR** ROOM.

WHAT'S IN **THERE**?

CRAWLSPACE. CONNECTS TO THE NEXT ROOM.

MAKE YOURSELF USEFUL AND STACK THOSE BOXES IN THE CORNER THERE.

I'M SO GLAD DAD BROUGHT THE CAT HOME.

YOU KNOW YOUR **FATHER.** CAN'T TURN AWAY A STRAY.

WHY DID HE CALL HIM **TUFF-TUFF?**

I DON'T KNOW, BECAUSE HE'S TOUGH, I SUPPOSE.

DID YOU REALLY NAME **ME** AFTER THE PETS?

MIDNIGHT, DAYLIGHT AND DAWN! HAHA NO...

THAT'S JUST A JOKE OF OURS.

OH.

HE SURE LOOKS A LOT LIKE **DAYLIGHT.**

POOR DAYLIGHT.

POISONED. REMEMBER?

UM...YEAH...

LYING UNDER THE FRONT PORCH, JUST... **DEAD.** NOTHING WRONG WITH THAT CAT.

SOMEONE **MUST** HAVE **POISONED** HIM, IT'S THE ONLY EXPLANATION.

DOES THIS **HAVE** TO BE MY ROOM?

JULY, 1971

Everyone had their favourite meal.

SIGH.

SKRAK!

DAWN! SUPPER!

DIDN'T COOK MIDNIGHT HIS **LIVER** TODAY.

YOU'RE NOT EATING THE **SKIN**? THE BEST PART? WHAT'S THE **MATTER** WITH YOU?

I DON'T LIKE IT, IT'S...

FER CHRIST'S SAKE.

YOU GOTTA PUT MORE **SALT** ON IT...

WHAT WAS **THAT**?

YIP! YAP!

IT'S A **GODDAMN BAT!**

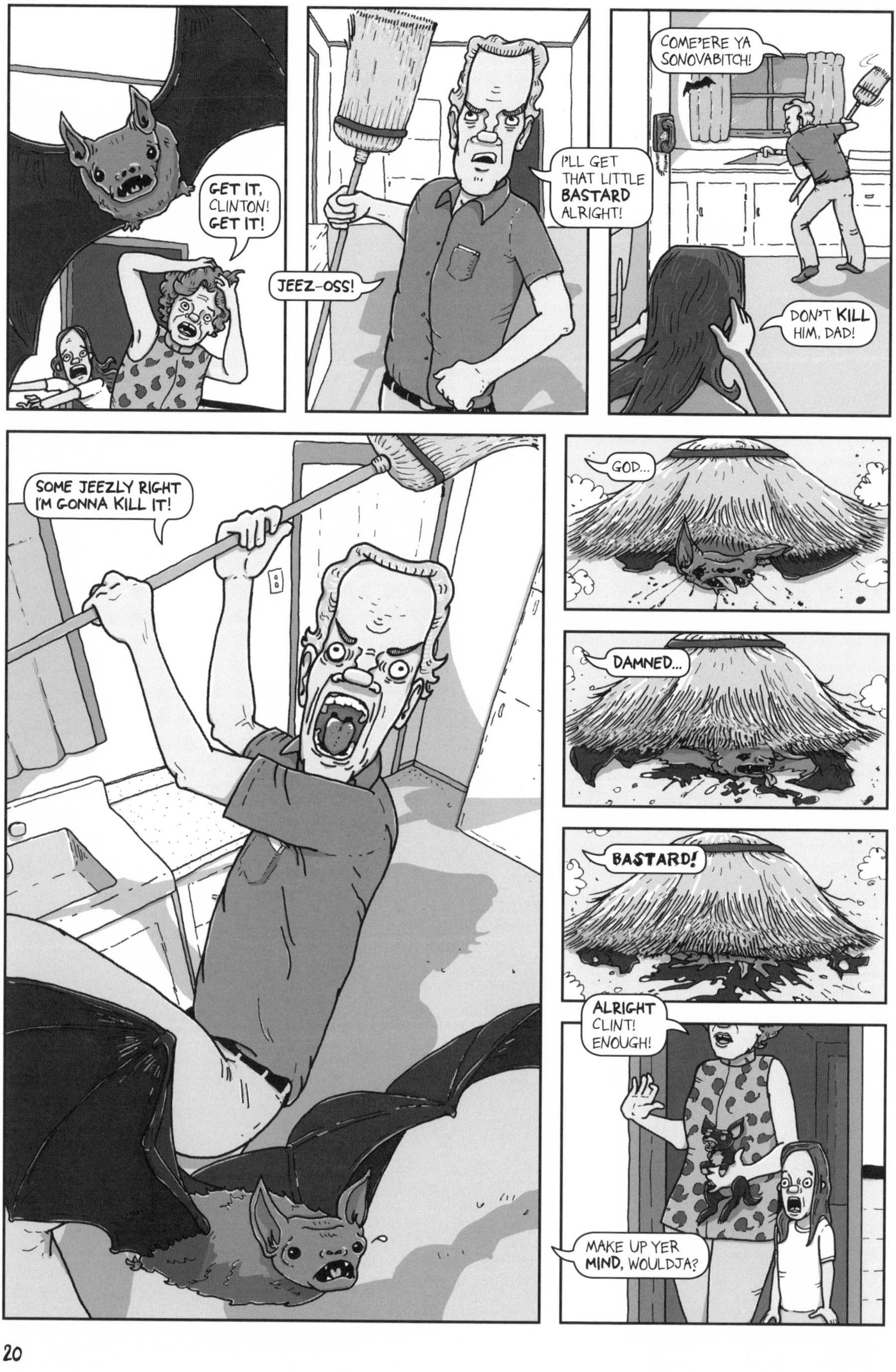
GET IT, CLINTON! GET IT!
JEEZ-OSS!
I'LL GET THAT LITTLE BASTARD ALRIGHT!
COME'ERE YA SONOVABITCH!
DON'T KILL HIM, DAD!
SOME JEEZLY RIGHT I'M GONNA KILL IT!
GOD...
DAMNED...
BASTARD!
ALRIGHT CLINT! ENOUGH!
MAKE UP YER MIND, WOULDJA?

GRADE ONE

PUT YOUR BOOKS AWAY.

SEPTEMBER, 1971

OKAY, CHILDREN...

TIME TO TEST YOUR **SKILLS.**

I'M GOING TO HOLD UP THESE **ANIMAL CARDS** AND YOU TELL ME WHAT **NOISE** THEY MAKE.

MEOW!

MEOW!

MEOW!

MEOW!

MOO!

MOO!

QUACK!

QUACK.

QUACK!

OINK!

OINK!

23

OINK!

HAVE YOU EVER ACTUALLY HEARD A PIG GO OINK OINK? THEY GO SNORT, GRUNT!

SQUEE!

TITTER!

GRUNT! SNORT!

NO, IT'S TRUE!

THEY DON'T GO OINK OINK, THEY GO GRUNT, SNORT.

DO YOU HAVE SOMETHING YOU'D LIKE TO SHARE WITH THE CLASSROOM, DAWN?

BUT... I WAS ONLY...

IT'S NOT POLITE TO MAKE FUN OF OTHERS.

GO STAND IN THE CORNER AND THINK ABOUT THAT FOR A WHILE.

BUT...

BA-A!

BAAA!

BAA!

BA-AA!

BAAA!

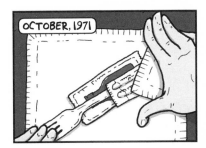

OCTOBER, 1971

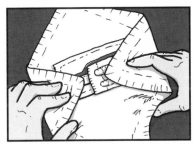

HOW MANY HAVE YOU DONE NOW? COUNT 'EM.

ONE CENT FOR EVERY NAPKIN.

RITA			✓		
VIVIAN			✓		
HELGA		✓			
ANNIE			✓		
EDITH					
JUDY	✓				

DON'T FORGET TO CHARGE AN EXTRA **THIRTY CENTS** FOR THOSE SCALLOPS.

30 CENTS!

WELL?

25.

GIVE 'EM TO YOUR AUNT VIV AND LET'S GO.

NICE WORK, DEAR.

WAIT FOR **ME**!

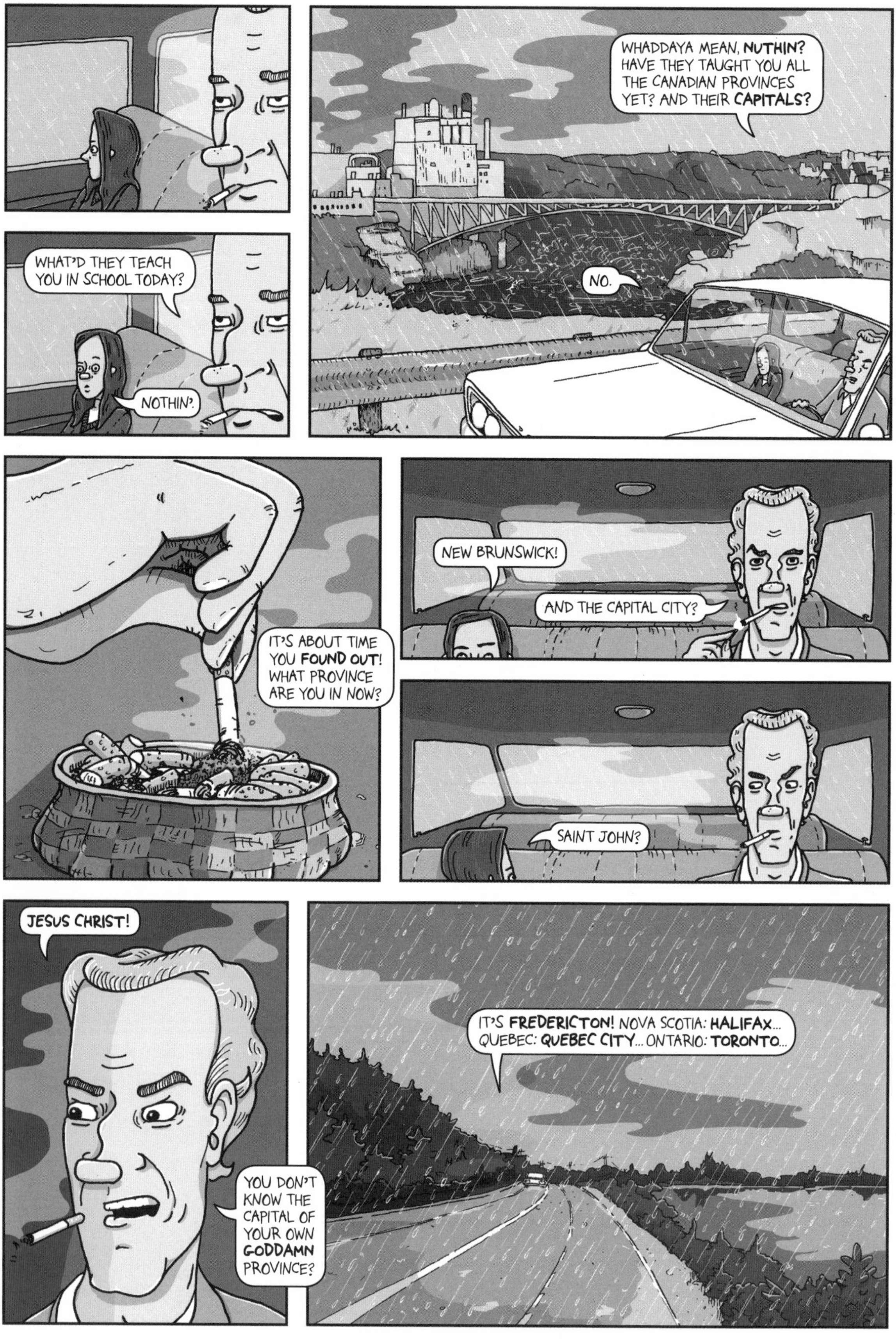
WHAT'D THEY TEACH YOU IN SCHOOL TODAY?
NOTHIN'.
WHADDAYA MEAN, **NUTHIN?** HAVE THEY TAUGHT YOU ALL THE CANADIAN PROVINCES YET? AND THEIR **CAPITALS?**
NO.
IT'S ABOUT TIME YOU **FOUND OUT!** WHAT PROVINCE ARE YOU IN NOW?
NEW BRUNSWICK!
AND THE CAPITAL CITY?
SAINT JOHN?
JESUS CHRIST!
YOU DON'T KNOW THE CAPITAL OF YOUR OWN **GODDAMN** PROVINCE?
IT'S **FREDERICTON!** NOVA SCOTIA: **HALIFAX**... QUEBEC: **QUEBEC CITY**... ONTARIO: **TORONTO**...

DECEMBER, 1971

HEY, ANYONE WANT SOME **FREE MONEY**?

YEAH!

WOAH!

I DO!

I GOT **40** CENTS!

I GOT **55!**

DO YOU HAVE ANY **MORE**?

WHAT'S **GOING ON** HERE?

SHE'S THROWING AWAY **MONEY!**

GIVE IT BACK. **ALL** OF IT.

DAWN, WHAT ON **EARTH** WERE YOU **THINKING**?

YOU OUGHT TO BE **ASHAMED** OF YOURSELF.

WAIT 'TIL YOU HEAR WHAT YOUR DAUGHTER DID AT SCHOOL TODAY.

SHE THREW A HANDFUL OF **MONEY** INTO THE AIR TO IMPRESS THE OTHER KIDS.

JESUS CHRIST ALMIGHTY!

THROWIN' **MONEY** AROUND! WHAT IN THE **HELL'S WRONG** WITH YA?

TRYING TO **BUY** FRIENDS.

WHERE'D YOU **GET** THAT MONEY?

ROLLING NAPKINS.

I WON'T DO IT AGAIN.

DAMN RIGHT YOU WON'T.

I'LL TEACH YOU THE VALUE OF **MONEY**!

NOW, DAWN...

SPARE THE **ROD**, SPOIL THE **CHILD**!

YOU'LL THANK US FOR THIS ONE DAY.

JANUARY, 1972

HE'S A HARD-LOOKIN' TICKET.

YOU COULD HAVE PACKED THAT SNOW A BIT TIGHTER.

LOOK, HE'S LOPSIDED THERE, **FIX** THAT.

IF YOU'RE GOING TO **DO** SOMETHING, DO IT **RIGHT**.

SERVES YOU **RIGHT**. THAT'S WHAT YOU GET FOR BEING SO IMPATIENT.

FEBRUARY, 1972

I DON'T KNOW WHY YOU DON'T **PLAY** WITH THESE **DOLLS**.

I HAVE **NIGHTMARES** ABOUT THEM SOMETIMES.

I LIKE STUFFED ANIMALS.

I GET YOU ONE EVERY... LOOKIT THIS ONE YOU GOT FOR CHRISTMAS, IT'S NOT EVEN OUT OF THE **BOX**!

I WANTED A CHEMISTRY SET.

YOU'RE TOO YOUNG FOR THAT! BLOW THE **PLACE** UP.

WHAT ABOUT A TELESCOPE? OR MAYBE A MICROSCOPE?

I DON'T KNOW WHAT'S **WRONG** WITH YOU. WHY DON'T YOU LIKE THINGS FOR **LITTLE GIRLS**?

DON'T WANT YOU TO TURN OUT TO BE A **TOMBOY**.

THEN WHAT ABOUT AN EASY-BAKE OVEN?

YOU'RE TOO YOUNG FOR THAT, TOO. BURN THE PLACE **DOWN**!

MARCH, 1972

DID YOU FINISH YOUR ORANGES?

YES.

BE GOOD NOW.

AND TELL YOUR **FATHER** TO COME SEE ME MORE OFTEN.

THANKS FOR LUNCH, GRAM.

IN THE CHILL OF NIGHT, AT THE SCENE OF A CRIME, LIKE A STREAK OF LIGHT...

HE ARRIVES JUST IN TIME.

STINK-EEE! STINK-EEE!

GOTCHER **HAT**, STINKY!

HEY! GIVE IT **BACK**!

HAW!

SO UGLY SHE CAN'T STAND UP!

HAA!

HAHAHA!

STOP! STOP!

HAW!

HERE'S YOUR STUPID UGLY HAT, STINKY.

32

MAY, 1972

DAD, WHAT'S THAT BUILDING, ANYWAY?

THE LODGE. THEY HAVE DANCES AND PARTIES THERE AND THINGS LIKE THAT.

CAN WE GO INSIDE?

NO.

LOOK AT YOUR LINE! YOU GOT ONE! REEL HIM IN!

YOU'RE GONNA LOSE HIM! HERE, GIMME THAT!

33

OH NO, THE **POOR FISH**! DON'T **KILL** HIM!

WHAT'D YA THINK WE WERE **OUT HERE** FOR?

BUT BUT, IT'S **CRUEL**! NOW HE CAN'T BREATHE!

JESUS CHRIST ALMIGHTY. ALRIGHT, I'LL GIVE HIM SOME **WATER**.

SO, DID YOU TWO CATCH ANYTHING?

YOUR DAUGHTER HOOKED ONE, NOW SHE DOESN'T WANT TO **KILL** IT. JEESH.

I DON'T KNOW WHAT'S **WRONG** WITH YAHS.

CAN I **FEED** HIM? CAN WE NURSE HIM BACK TO **HEALTH**?

PLEASE!

I'LL FILL THE TUB.

CAN'T DO ANYTHING **RIGHT**.

35

JUNE, 1972

I'M VERY **DISAPPOINTED** IN YOU.

PRIMARY SCHOOL
GRADES 1 TO 3
1971 – 1972

OGRESS REPORT

BEING PUT IN THE **CORNER** FOR BEING DIS-RESPECTFUL...

BUT THAT WASN'T **FAIR!** I WAS ONLY...

AND BUYING FRIENDS... **WHY?** WHY CAN'T YOU MAKE ANY FRIENDS?

I DON'T KNOW WHERE YOU GET THAT **DAMN SHYNESS** FROM BUT...

YOU'RE GONNA HAFTA **GET OVER IT! AND...**

YOU'RE NOT **TRYING** HARD ENOUGH IN MATH.

JUST BEING **CARELESS!**

LANGUAGE ARTS
LETTER RECOGNITION
WORD RECOGNITION
READING COMPREHENSION
ORAL READING
ORAL EXPRESSION
SPELLING

MATHEMATICS

ALSO... SHE SAYS ALL YOU DRAW OR WRITE ABOUT IS **CATS.** DRAW SOMETHING ELSE!

JULY, 1972

I **STILL** DON'T GET IT.

WARM HOOMIN UNDERSTANDIN'?...

DR. DOLITTLEGOOD. THAT'S FUNNY BECAUSE IT'S LIKE DR. DOLITTLE...

BUT HE DOESN'T DO GOOD, SO HE'S DR. DO-LITTLE-GOOD, **SEE?**

THE PERFECT PLACE FOR ME AND **ALL** MY FRIENDS!

37

AUGUST, 1972

CHICKEN FOR EVERYONE!

ARLENE PROBABLY BROUGHT TODD. HE'S YOUR AGE.

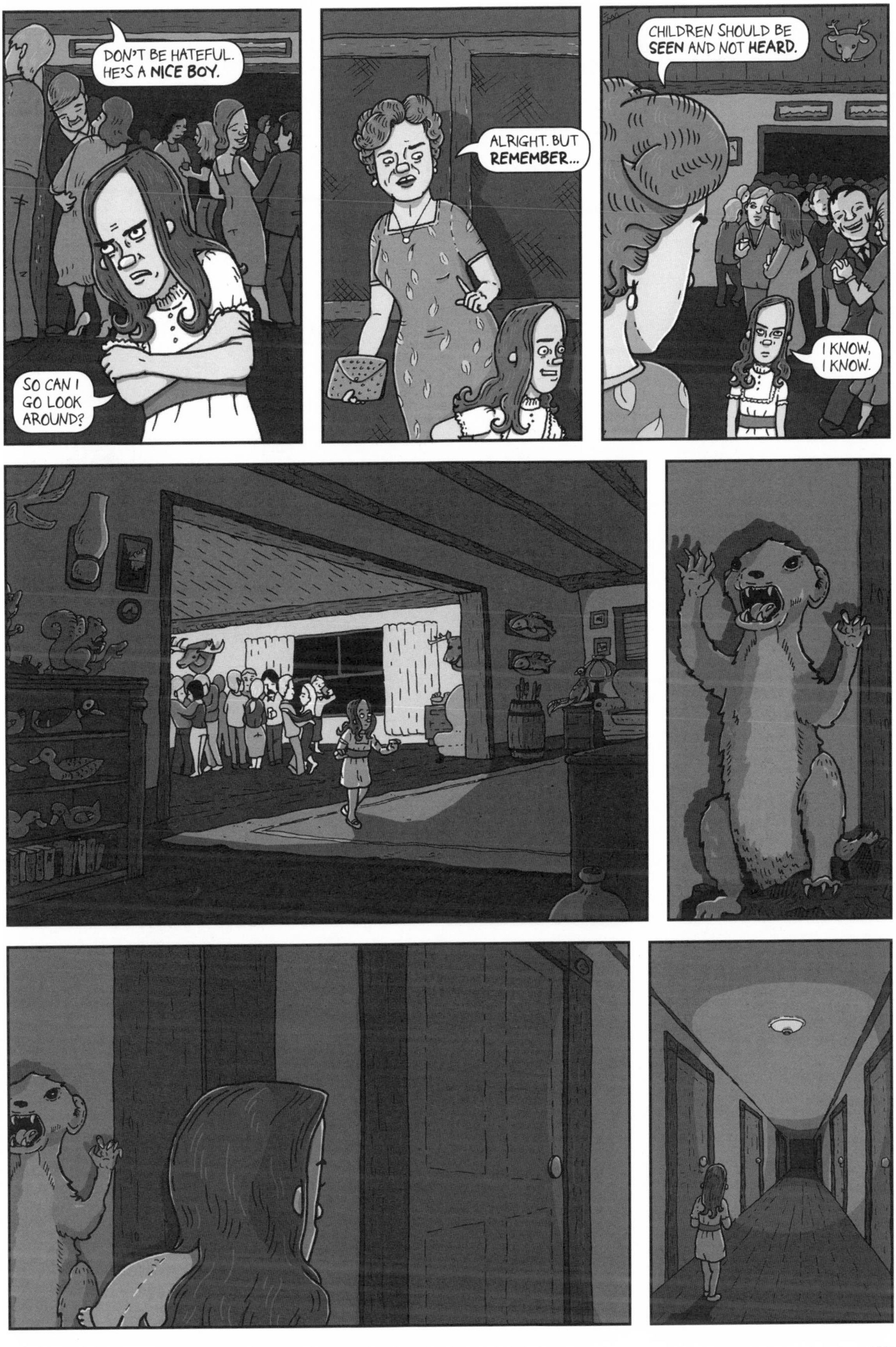
DON'T BE HATEFUL. HE'S A NICE BOY.
SO CAN I GO LOOK AROUND?
ALRIGHT. BUT REMEMBER...
CHILDREN SHOULD BE SEEN AND NOT HEARD.
I KNOW, I KNOW.

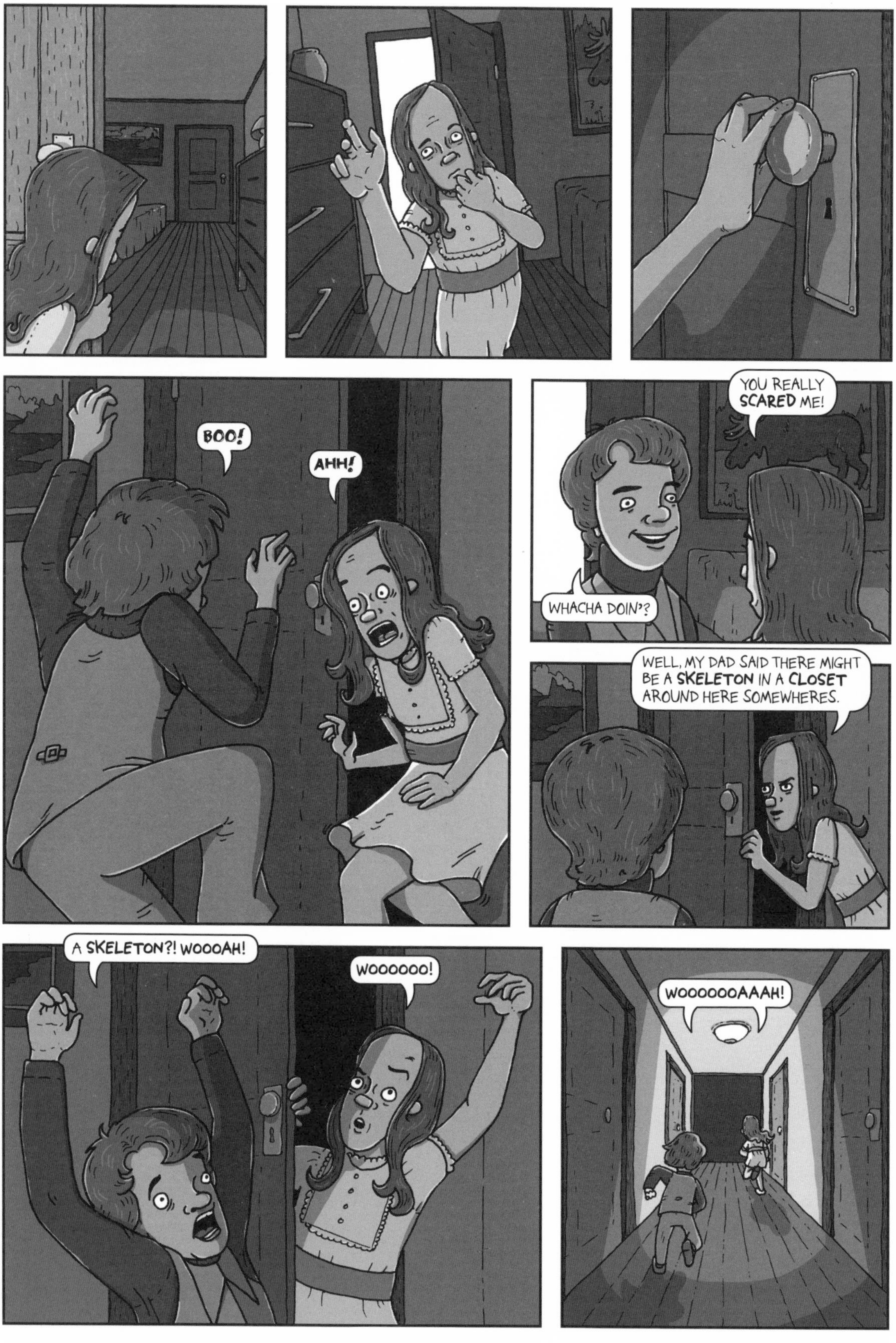
BOO!
AHH!
YOU REALLY SCARED ME!
WHACHA DOIN'?
WELL, MY DAD SAID THERE MIGHT BE A SKELETON IN A CLOSET AROUND HERE SOMEWHERES.
A SKELETON?! WOOOAH!
WOOOOOO!
WOOOOOOAAAH!

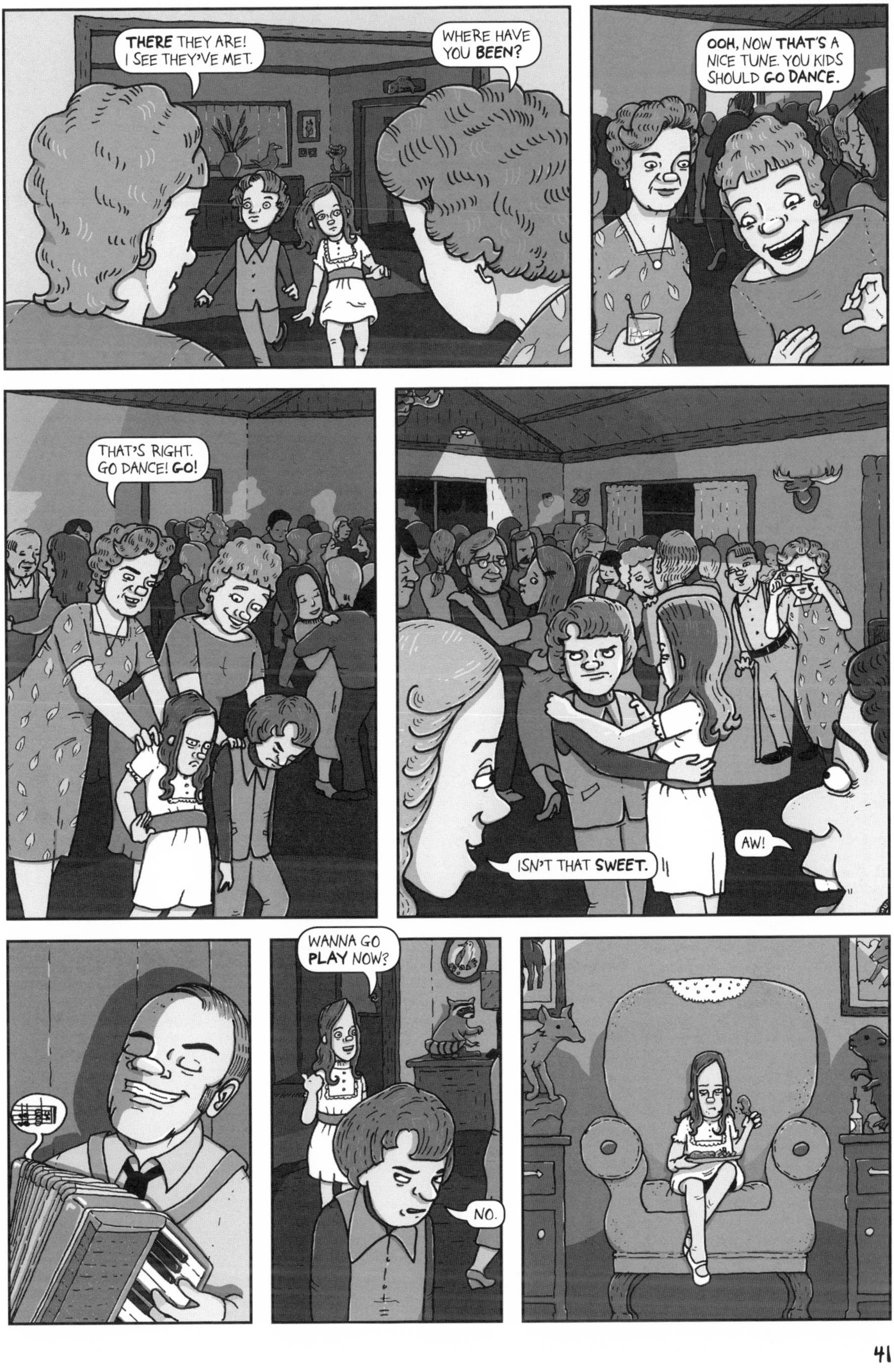
THERE THEY ARE! I SEE THEY'VE MET.
WHERE HAVE YOU BEEN?
OOH, NOW THAT'S A NICE TUNE. YOU KIDS SHOULD GO DANCE.
THAT'S RIGHT. GO DANCE! GO!
ISN'T THAT SWEET.
AW!
WANNA GO PLAY NOW?
NO.

GRADE TWO

SEPTEMBER, 1972

SO I DECIDED I WANT TO BE AN **ARTIST** WHEN I GROW UP.

DON'T BE **RIDICULOUS.** YOU DON'T WANT TO BE AN ARTIST.

YOU'LL **STARVE.** WHY DO YOU THINK THEY CALL THEM **STARVING ARTISTS**?

WHY ARE YOU COLOURING IT UP AND DOWN LIKE THAT?

TEACHER SAYS I HAVE TO DO IT LIKE THIS...

OH **NO, NO, NO!** SHE DOESN'T KNOW WHAT SHE'S TALKING ABOUT. HERE.

ROUND YOUR STROKES LIKE THIS. IT SHOULD **FEEL** LIKE WHAT IT IS.

BUT TEACHER SAYS...

I DON'T **CARE** WHAT YOUR TEACHER SAYS. SHE'S WRONG.

AND THAT'S NOT HOW YOU DRAW A TREE, EITHER!

FASCINATING, CAPTAIN.

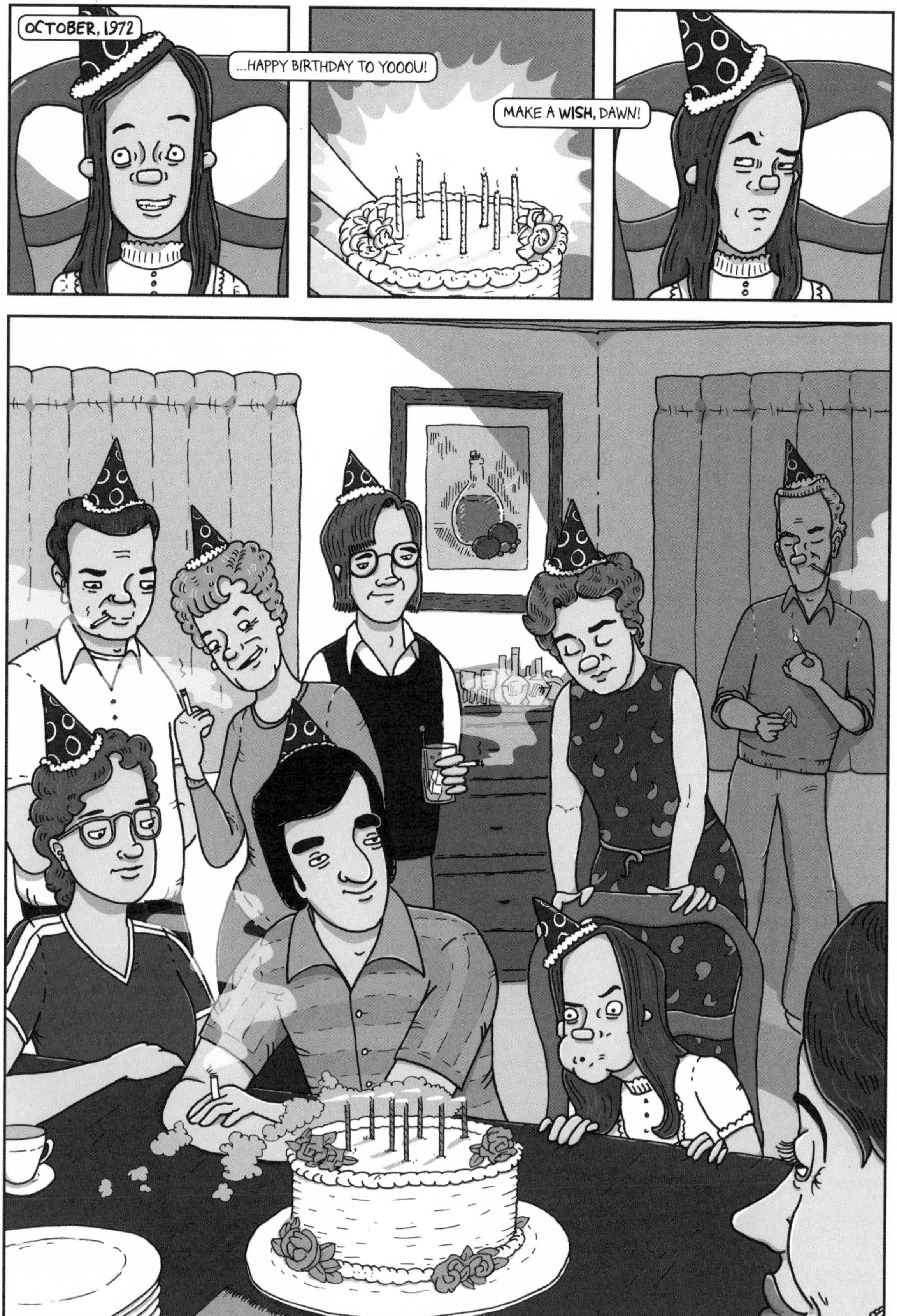
OCTOBER, 1972
...HAPPY BIRTHDAY TO YOOOU!
MAKE A WISH, DAWN!

OCTOBER, 1972

THE TARLOST

YOU'VE DONE ALL YOUR HOMEWORK?

YES MOM.

WHAT'S 8 X 7? QUICK!

54?

56! YOU SHOULD KNOW OFF THE TOP OF YOUR **HEAD!** GO WRITE OUT YOUR MULTIPLICATION TABLES. THREE TIMES. **NOW.**

MO-O-M! SHOW'S ALMOST OVER!

AFTER THE SHOW.

THE LEAST YOU COULD DO IS SAY HI DOG, HOW ARE YA?

I HOPE YOU REMEMBERED THE MILK. CLINTON, DO YOU EVEN **HEAR** ME?

JESUS CHRIST! YES, YES, YES, GIMME A BREAK!

JUST LIKE HIS MOTHER. **SELECTIVE HEARING.**

AFTER TEACHING A ROOMFUL OF **KIDS** ALL DAY LONG, YOU **BET** I DO.

DO YOU HAVE AN **EXCEDRIN** HEADACHE?

47

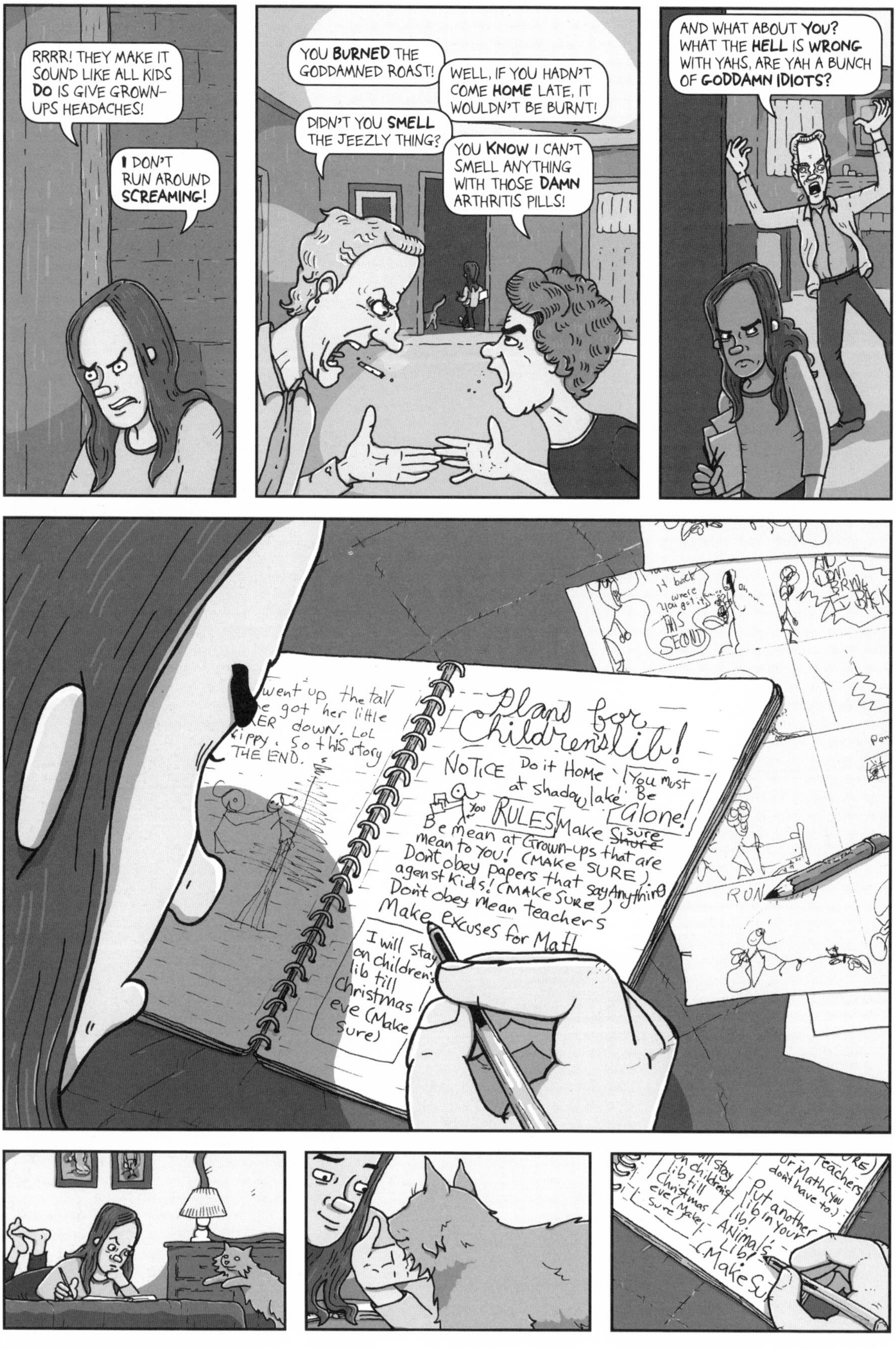
RRRR! THEY MAKE IT SOUND LIKE ALL KIDS DO IS GIVE GROWN-UPS HEADACHES!
I DON'T RUN AROUND SCREAMING!
YOU BURNED THE GODDAMNED ROAST!
DIDN'T YOU SMELL THE JEEZLY THING?
WELL, IF YOU HADN'T COME HOME LATE, IT WOULDN'T BE BURNT!
YOU KNOW I CAN'T SMELL ANYTHING WITH THOSE DAMN ARTHRITIS PILLS!
AND WHAT ABOUT YOU? WHAT THE HELL IS WRONG WITH YAHS, ARE YAH A BUNCH OF GODDAMN IDIOTS?
went up the tall
e got her little
ER down. LoL
ippy. So this story
THE END.
it back where you got it
THIS SECOND
RUN
Plans for Children's lib!
NOTICE
Do it Home at shadow lake
You must Be Alone!
You
RULES
Make sure
Be mean at Grown-ups that are mean to you! (MAKE SURE)
Don't obey papers that say Anything agenst kids! (MAKE SURE)
Don't obey mean teachers
Make excuses for Math
I will stay on children's lib till Christmas eve (Make sure)
stay
on children's
lib till
Christmas
eve (Make
sure)
teachers
or Math (you don't have to.)
Put another lib in your lib!
ANimals Lib!
(Make Su

NOVEMBER, 1972

ALRIGHT CHILDREN, TIME FOR YOUR **MATH** TEST!

WHAT IS IT, DAWN?

I DON'T **FEEL** VERY GOOD. I HAVE A STOMACH ACHE.

OH? **AGAIN?**

I THINK I NEED TO GO TO THE **SICK ROOM.**

HMM. YOU DON'T LOOK **SICK** TO ME.

BUT I REALLY **DO** FEEL **BAD!**

WE'LL **SEE** ABOUT THAT. NOW TAKE YOUR SEAT.

49

HIGH STICK TO THE FACE! HE'S GOIN' TO **THE BOX** FOR THAT ONE!

I HAVE A **BONE** TO PICK WITH YOU.

I JUST HEARD YOU'VE BEEN **LYING!** LYING TO GET OUT OF **MATH CLASS!**

I WASN'T LYING! I **DID** FEEL **SICK!**

MY OWN DAUGHTER! A GODDAMN **LIAR!**

I'M **NOT!** MATH MAKES ME FEEL **REALLY BAD!**

I THOUGHT I WAS RAISING YOU **RIGHT** BUT I GUESS I WENT **WRONG** SOMEWHERES.

CAN'T DO ANYTHING **RIGHT.**

AND WHERE DO YOU THINK **YOU'RE** GOING? YOU **KNOW** YOU DESERVE IT!

MAYBE **THIS**'LL POUND SOME **SENSE** INTO YA!

NOW DON'T BE LIKE THAT. YOU WOULDN'T WANT US TO BE LIKE THOSE **PERMISSIVE PARENTS** WHO DON'T **CARE** ABOUT THEIR CHILDREN, WOULD YOU?

WOULD YOU??

51

DECEMBER, 1972

...YOOOU CAN COUNT ON ME...

WHERE THE **HELL** IS YOUR FATHER?

ELVIS CHRISTMAS ALBUM

CHRISTMAS **EVE** FOR CHRISTSAKES.

LOOK, YOU HAVE A BUNCH OF BLUE ONES ALL IN **ONE SPOT.** SPREAD THEM OUT.

AND THE BIG ONES SHOULD GO IN BACK.

NO, DEAR. YOU DON'T HAVE THE **PATIENCE** FOR IT. YOU HAVE TO DO IT **ONE STRAND** AT A TIME.

CAN I PUT **TINSEL** ON?

ABOUT **TIME!**

GET OFF MY **BACK** WILL YA! I JUST **WALKED** THROUGH THE **DOOR.**

I WAS WORRIED! I COULDN'T GET THROUGH. THE **PARTY LINE** WAS BUSY ALL NIGHT!

WE SHOULD **MOVE.**

DID YOU BRING **CHICKEN** AND A **PEPSI** TO LEAVE OUT FOR SANTA?

I SURE DID!

MOM! THE CONDUCTOR'S COMING! HIDE **MIDNIGHT!**

HE WON'T SAY ANYTHING. HE KNOWS ME FROM THE DAYS I WORKED FOR **C.N.**

SYBIL! WELL! ÇA VA **BIEN?!** NOW WHERE ARE YOU HEADED IN THIS COLD?

BONSOIR ALAIN! SEEM TO MISS CAMPBELLTON 'ROUND THIS TIME OF YEAR.

C'EST MA FILLE, DAWN.

BONSOIR!

HI. UH, BONSWAR.

I SEE YOU STILL HAVE TON P'TIT **D'JÂB DE PURSE!**

GRRR!

TRÈS DRÔLE! HAHA!

ALORS, BON VOYAGE! IT IS GOOD TO HAVE YOU BACK UP NORTH WITH US!

53

HE WAS NICE.

OH YES. NICE FELLA, THAT ALAIN.

WHY DON'T YOU SPEAK FRENCH AT HOME?

WELL...

SOME PEOPLE DON'T CARE FOR IT, YOU KNOW... THAT I WAS A FRENCH CATHOLIC.

WHAT DIFFERENCE DOES THAT MAKE?

WELL, IT SHOULDN'T MAKE ANY DIFFERENCE. BUT IT DOES TO SOME PEOPLE.

WHY?

SIGH. THAT'S WHAT PEOPLE ARE LIKE. YOU'LL FIND OUT AS YOU GROW UP.

AND IF YOU EVER CATCH ME SAYING ANYTHING WITH A FRENCH ACCENT, YOU MAKE SURE TO LET ME KNOW!

MARCH, 1973

SIGH.

I THOUGHT YOU **LIKED** BLACKOUTS.

YEAH BUT I WISH I KNEW HOW THAT **MOVIE** ENDED.

DAVID NIVEN WAS REALLY FUNNY AS THAT **GHOST**. I LIKE COMEDIANS.

WELL, DAVID NIVEN ISN'T A COMEDIAN **PER SE**...

I DECIDED **I** WANT TO BE A **COMEDIAN** WHEN I GROW UP.

WHAT WOULD YOU WANT TO DO **THAT** FOR?

WELL... JERRY LEWIS AND **GILLIGAN**...

BOB DENVER.

BOB DENVER... **THEY'RE** REALLY FUNNY... I COULD BE LIKE **THAT**.

NO, NO, NO. YOU DON'T WANT TO DO **THAT**.

COMEDIANS ARE ACTUALLY QUITE **SAD** PEOPLE, YOU KNOW. MOST OF THEM DON'T MAKE IT. IT'S A **VERY** HARD LIFE.

BESIDES, YOU'D HAVE TO GET OVER THAT DAMNED **SHYNESS** OF YOURS.

I'M ONLY SAYING THIS BECAUSE I **LOVE** YOU.

A LITTLE WHITE ON TOP WHERE THE **LIGHT** WOULD HIT IT... A LITTLE BLACK UNDERNEATH FOR THE SHADOW... SEE? NOW **YOU** TRY IT.

NOT BAD.

SEE, YOU DON'T HAVE TO DO SOMETHING **EXACTLY** TO GET THE IDEA ACROSS.

BUT SOME THINGS HAVE TO BE EXACT, RIGHT?

RIGHT. LIKE TINSEL.

LIKE TINSEL?

JUNE, 1973

ISN'T SHE PRETTY?

SO HOW LONG ARE YOU STAYING, VEGA?

A COUPLE OF WEEKS I GUESS.

WE COME TO GRAMPY'S CAMP **EVERY** SUMMER.

SO WE CAN PLAY **EVERY DAY!**

LOOKIT HER DRESS, IT'S NEW. MOMMY BOUGHT IT FOR ME.

YOU WANNA COME SEE MY **SECRET HEADQUARTERS?**

NO. LET'S GO OVER THERE.

WHEN I GROW UP, I WANT TO BE A **HAIRDRESSER.**

I WANT TO BE AN ART...

OR MAYBE A FASHION MODEL. I THINK I'D BE PRETTY GOOD AT THAT.

GET TO WEAR LOTS OF PRETTY CLOTHES...

WOAH! LOOK!

EWWW!

CAT MUSTA GOT IT!

IT'S DISGUSTING.

LET'S GO TO THE LAKE!

BUT... I'M STILL LOOKING.

IF YOU DON'T COME WITH ME, I WON'T BE YOUR FRIEND.

JULY, 1973

WHO IS **THIS?**

THAT'S **KAREN.** YOUR **HALF-SISTER.** FROM YOUR FATHER'S FIRST MARRIAGE AFTER THE WAR. SHE'D BE IN HER MID-**TWENTIES** NOW.

TWENTIES!

Electrolux

OH YES. I WAS WORRIED, YOU KNOW, WHEN I HAD YOU. THOUGHT IT WAS **TOO LATE IN LIFE** TO HAVE A BABY.

YOU TURNED OUT TO BE THE **BEST THING** THAT EVER HAPPENED TO ME.

BUT I STILL GET PEOPLE TELLING ME WHAT A **'LOVELY GRANDDAUGHTER'** I HAVE!

IT'S LIKE WE HAVE **TWO GENERATION GAPS!**

59

IS THAT YOU WHEN **YOU** WERE LITTLE?

THOSE WERE MY **BROTHERS!**

THEY USED TO MAKE BOYS LOOK LIKE LITTLE GIRLS BACK THEN...

MADE THEM LOOK LIKE **ANGELS.**

HAHA! UNCLE FRANK LOOKED LIKE **THAT?**

NO, THESE WERE MY **OLDER BROTHERS.** THEY **DROWNED.**

DROWNED?

OH YES. LITTLE SANFORD CHASED HIS HOOP OUT ONTO THE **ICE** AND **FELL THROUGH.** GORDON, BLESS HIS HEART, RAN TO **SAVE** HIM BUT...

THEY BOTH **DIED.**

I WATCHED IT ALL HAPPEN. I WAS ONLY **FOUR** BUT I CAN STILL SEE IT LIKE IT WAS **YESTERDAY.**

DID IT MAKE YOU REALLY **SAD?** DO YOU MISS THEM?

ALONE

OH, THAT'S ALL IN THE **PAST,** IT DOESN'T HAVE MUCH EFFECT **ANY MORE.**

60

AUGUST, 1973

GET OUTTA HERE, WILL YA!

I KNOW THAT WAS PRETTY **SCARY**...

BUT YOU'LL LIKE **THIS**, AMANDA!

COOKIES ARE READY!

GIVE SOME TO YOUR COUSIN.

YOU CAN FEED THEM BY **HAND**!

WAIT 'TIL YOU SEE THEM!

YOU DON'T THINK THEY'RE **CUTE**?

SO WHEN'S MY **DAD** COMING TO PICK ME UP?

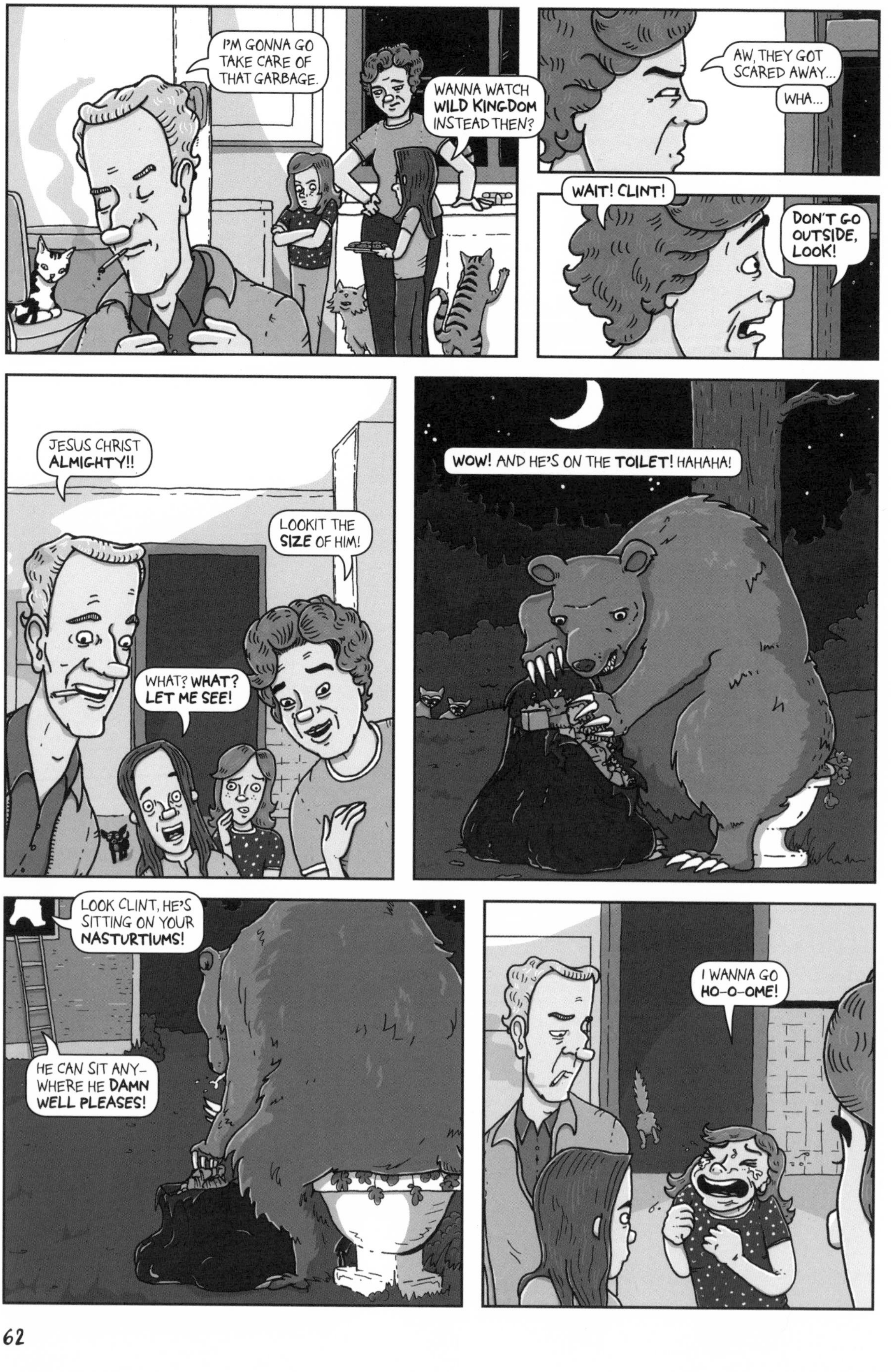
I'M GONNA GO TAKE CARE OF THAT GARBAGE.
WANNA WATCH **WILD KINGDOM** INSTEAD THEN?
AW, THEY GOT SCARED AWAY...
WHA...
WAIT! CLINT!
DON'T GO OUTSIDE, LOOK!
JESUS CHRIST **ALMIGHTY!!**
LOOKIT THE **SIZE** OF HIM!
WHAT? **WHAT? LET ME SEE!**
WOW! AND HE'S ON THE **TOILET!** HAHAHA!
LOOK CLINT, HE'S SITTING ON YOUR **NASTURTIUMS!**
HE CAN SIT ANY-WHERE HE **DAMN WELL PLEASES!**
I WANNA GO **HO-O-OME!**

GRADE THREE

SEPTEMBER, 1973

IT'S TOO **LATE** TO PLANT SEEDS. THOSE NASTURTIUMS WON'T HAVE TIME TO GROW!

BITE ME ARMPIT.

STUBBORN, JUST LIKE THE **REST** OF 'EM.

HARUMPH.

MOM...

I **STILL** CAN'T FIND TUFFY.

GO ASK MABEL AND CHARLEY. MAYBE THEY'VE SEEN HIM.

HE'S BEEN GONE FOR **THREE DAYS**!

HE'LL BE BACK!

TUFF-TUFF! HERE TUFFY! PSS PSS!

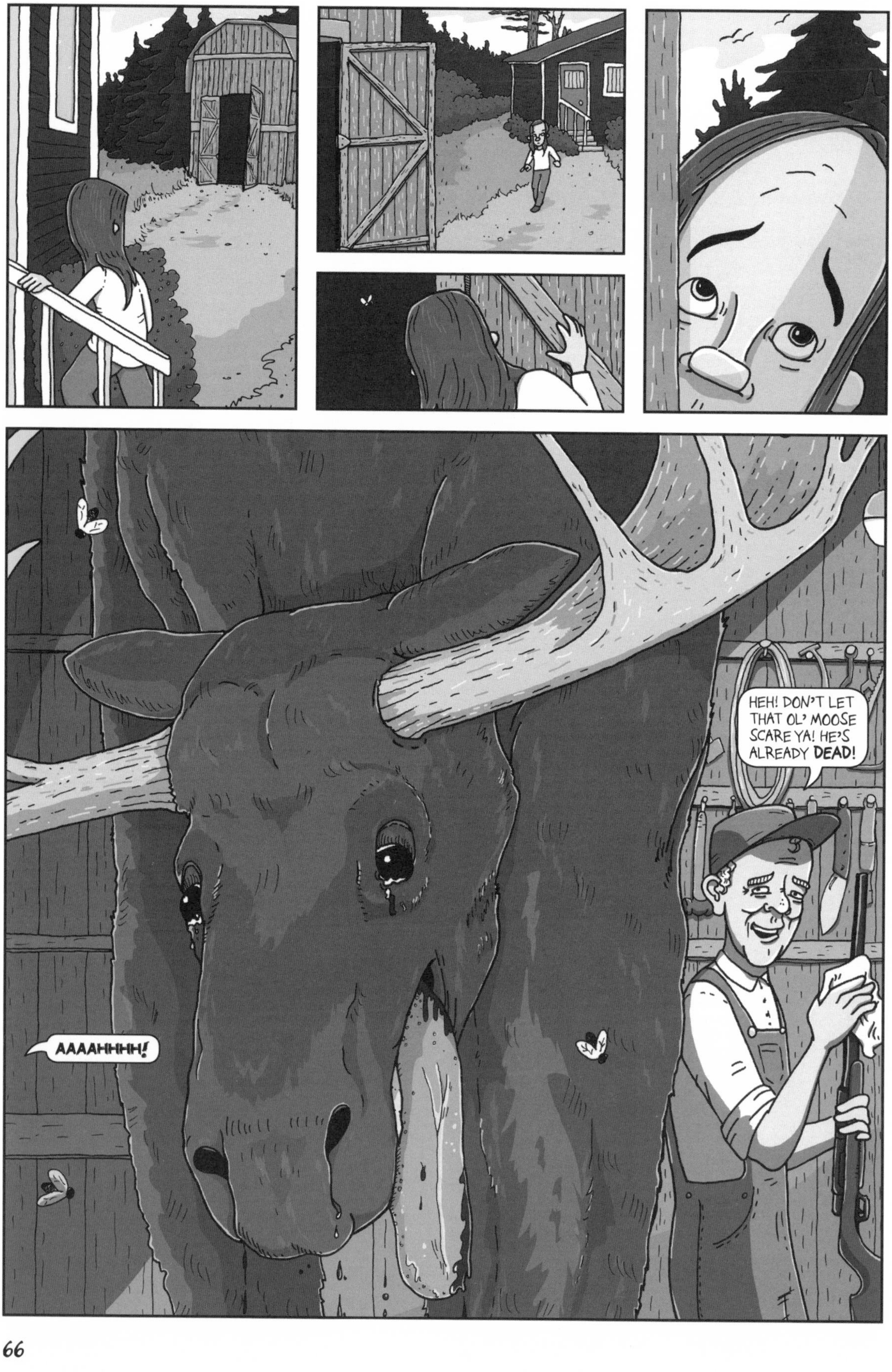
HEH! DON'T LET THAT OL' MOOSE SCARE YA! HE'S ALREADY **DEAD**!
AAAAHHHH!

OCTOBER, 1973

HE DIDN'T DO IT ON **PURPOSE!**

I KNOW.

IT WAS MY OWN DAMN FAULT. CAN'T DO ANYTHING RIGHT.

SO I DECIDED I WANT TO BE A **VET** WHEN I GROW UP.

OH, YOU **DON'T** WANT TO BE A VET.

YES I DO!

NO, YOU **DON'T.** AROUND ANIMALS **SUFFERING** ALL THE TIME...

NUMBER 31?

PUTTING ALL THOSE CATS AND DOGS TO **SLEEP**...YOUR **HEART** WOULD **BREAK.**

YOU REALLY SHOULD GET INTO **ARTHRITIS RESEARCH** SINCE YOU'RE PROBABLY GOING TO **GET IT TOO.**

67

SO, A **RACCOON** BITE, HUH? GOING TO NEED A **RABIES** SHOT.

THEY MAY LOOK **CUTE**, DEAR, BUT THEY CAN BE DANGEROUS!

BUT I'M NOT...

I'M THE ONE WHO GOT BITTEN.

OH! I JUST ASSUMED.

THE DOCTOR WILL BE WITH YOU SHORTLY.

WHY WOULD SHE **ASSUME** THAT? JUST BECAUSE I'M A **KID**? RRR!

IT'S JUST LIKE THOSE **EXCEDRIN** COMMERCIALS!

HA! THAT MAKES YOU SO **MAD**! THAT'S YOUR **MISPLACED PRIDE**, THAT.

OCTOBER, 1973

GOOD NIGHT, DEAR! WATCH OUT FOR GHOULS AND GOBLINS!

YOU SAID APPLES COULD HAVE **RAZOR BLADES** IN THEM AT HALLOWE'EN.

I DON'T THINK YOU HAVE TO WORRY ABOUT **MABEL**.

YOU SAID IT'S USUALLY THE PEOPLE YOU **TRUST**.

I WISH THERE WAS SOMEWHERES **ELSE** TO GO TRICK-OR-TREATING.

I KNOW. WELL... WE HAVE LOTS OF CANDY AT HOME. LET'S GO **HAVE** SOME AND WATCH A HORROR MOVIE.

YEAH!

NOVEMBER, 1973

MOM, I'M **SCARED**.

OF WHAT?

I'M SCARED OF DYING. I'M AFRAID TO **DIE**!

THAT'S **RIDICULOUS**. IT'S JUST THE **MUMPS**.

NO, NO, I MEAN... I'M GONNA **DIE** ONE DAY. AND THERE'S **NOTHING** I CAN **DO ABOUT IT**!

NOW WHY ARE YOU THINKING ABOUT **THAT**?

I THINK ABOUT IT **ALL** THE **TIME**.

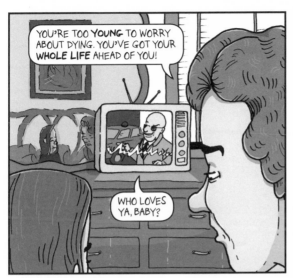

YOU'RE TOO **YOUNG** TO WORRY ABOUT DYING. YOU'VE GOT YOUR **WHOLE LIFE** AHEAD OF YOU!

WHO LOVES YA, BABY?

I'LL GO FIND SOME **CANDLES**.

LISTEN TO THAT **WIND**.

EVERYTIME I HEAR THE WIND I THINK OF MY **MOTHER**. SHE THOUGHT IT WAS THE. **SADDEST SOUND** IN THE WORLD.

SHE USED TO RECITE THIS POEM...

HAVE YOU EVER HEARD THE WIND GO **YOOOO**? 'TIS A **PITIFUL** SOUND TO HEAR!
IT SEEMS TO CHILL YOU THROUGH AND THROUGH WITH A **STRANGE** AND SPEECHLESS FEAR...
AND THEN SOMETHING LIKE...
THE NIGHT WOULD SAY IN ITS GHOSTLY WAY: YOU! **YOOU! YOOOOOOOOU!**

YOU WOULD HAVE **LIKED** MY MOTHER.

71

JANUARY, 1974

CLIP YOUR TOENAILS, MIDNIGHT? HUH? CLIP YOUR TOENAILS?

GRRR!

HE HATES IT WHEN YOU SAY THAT.

HAHA!

SO I FIRED JUDY TODAY.

GOOD. NOTHING BUT TROUBLE. MUST HAVE BEEN HARD TO DO.

I TOLD HER THERE'S NO CHANGING YOUR MIND.

NOT REALLY. I TOLD HER IT WAS **YOUR** IDEA.

WHAT?

YOU DIDN'T WANT TO LOOK BAD SO YOU MADE **ME** THE BAD GUY?

WHAT DO YOU CARE WHAT THEY THINK OF YOU?

HYPOCRITE.

Cats are cute
This one plays a flute
With a toot-toot-toot

I LIKE YOUR **CAT**.

THANKS.

I **LOVE** CATS. I HAVE A WHITE ONE.

WE HAD **THREE** BUT ONE **RAN AWAY**. AND WE HAVE A CHIHUAHUA BUT HE'S **SICK**.

WOW! DO YOU HAVE ANY BROTHERS OR SISTERS?

NO.

AW, NO FAIR! I HAVE **TWO** BROTHERS AND ONLY **ONE** CAT!

MY MOM SAYS **ALL** ONLY CHILDREN ARE **SPOILED ROTTEN**.

I'M NOT **SPOILED!**

YEAH **RIGHT.** LOTS OF PETS. ALL THE **FRIED CHICKEN** YOU WANT. RIGHT.

I'M NOT **SPOILED!**

ALRIGHT CHILDREN, SETTLE DOWN NOW.

73

MARCH, 1974

ALL THAT'S **LEFT** IS HIS LITTLE BLANKET.

AT LEAST HE'S NOT SUFFERING ANYMORE.

I'M GOING TO **MISS** HIM SO MUCH.

OH, DAWN. WHAT AM I GOING TO **DO?**

APRIL, 1974

STRUCK BY **LIGHTNING!** JESUS CHRIST ALMIGHTY!

GOD MUST BE TRYING TO TELL US SOMETHING! IT'S A GOOD THING WE'RE GOING TO SEE THAT HOUSE.

THE **GRASS** IS ON THE **ROOF!**

WHAT **HOUSE?**

BACK IN THE **CITY.**

WE'RE MOVING?

ONCE THE SCHOOL YEAR ENDS, YES.

ALL THAT DRIVING. WE'RE JUST TOO **FAR** FROM EVERYTHING OUT HERE.

BUT I **LOVE** SHADOW LAKE!

I KNOW, DEAR. BUT MAYBE YOU CAN MAKE SOME **FRIENDS** IF YOU'RE NOT IN THE MIDDLE OF **NOWHERE.**

BUT...

NO BUTS ABOUT IT.

APRIL, 1974

MOM!

LOOKIT MY MATH TEST!

99% Excellent!

99%? WHAT'S THE **POINT** OF GETTING 99%?

BUT SYB, THAT'S A **WONDERFUL** MARK!

DON'T ENCOURAGE HER, VIV. IF YOU CAN GET **THAT CLOSE** TO 100, YOU CAN GET 100.

SEE. IT'S YOUR OWN FAULT. CARELESSNESS!

IT WAS AN **ACCIDENT!**

THERE'S **NO SUCH THING** AS AN ACCIDENT.

LIKE **MY MOTHER** ALWAYS TOLD ME...

ACCIDENTS ARE **CAUSED BY STUPIDITY.**

MAY, 1974

ARE YOU PAYING ATTENTION TO THE **STORY**?

YES, MOM!

WON **SEVEN** OSCARS!

'ORRENCE!

IS IT **OVER**? IS IT **OVER**? AHHH! I CAN STILL **HEAR** IT! *LA LA LA*!

AAHH!

WHA... GASP!

AAHH!

OKAY, YOU CAN COME BACK IN. THE **COMMERCIAL'S** ON.

IS IT THAT **EXCEDRIN** COMMERCIAL?

KINDA SCARY, THAT BEHAVIOUR.

BUT IT'S SO **HORRIBLE**...

WELL, QUICKSAND IS ONE THING... BUT YOU GET UPSET WATCHING **COLUMBO**!

THAT GUY WAS BEING **FRAMED**! IT'S SO AWFUL! I CAN'T **WATCH** IT!

AND YOU'RE LIKE ME — YOU CAN'T WATCH THE **ANIMAL SHOWS**...

IT'S SO **CRUEL**! THERE'S ALWAYS SOME **HUNTER** WHO **KILLS** THEM!

THEY CAN'T DEFEND THEMSELVES! IT'S NOT **FAIR**! I **HATE** HUNTERS!

I WISH THE **ANIMALS** COULD GET **REVENGE** AND **TEAR THEM APART**!

ARGH!

AH HON. IT'S **GOOD** THAT THESE THINGS UPSET YOU... IT MEANS YOU HAVE A GOOD **HEART**. BUT YOU'RE GONNA HAVE A **HARD LIFE** BEING SO **SENSITIVE**.

YOU'VE GOT TO LET IT **ROLL OFF YOU** LIKE **WATER** OFF A DUCK'S BACK.

JUNE, 1974

BWWAAHH!

WHAT IS IT, DEAR? WHAT'S **WRONG**? ARE YOU **HURT**?

NO!

DID SOMEONE **DO** SOMETHING TO YOU?

NO!

I CAN'T **HELP** YOU IF YOU WON'T TELL ME WHAT'S **WRONG**!

I DON'T KNOW!!

BWWAAHH!

JULY, 1974

THIS CAN BE WHERE I SLEEP, BECAUSE I'M THE **MOMMY**, AND YOU SLEEP THERE, 'CUZ YOU'RE THE **LITTLE GIRL**.

AND **THIS** IS YOUR BIG SISTER.

WHY AM I THE LITTLE GIRL, VEGA?

WELL I SAID IT **FIRST**, SO YOU HAVE TO DO WHAT **I SAY**.

SO NOW YOU HAVE TO GET UP AND COME OVER TO THE KITCHEN 'CUZ I'M GONNA MAKE **BREAKFAST**.

I DON'T WANT TO PLAY THIS ANYMORE.

IF YOU **DON'T,** I WON'T BE YOUR **FRIEND.**

I'M **WARNING** YOU!

AUGUST, 1974

MANAWAGONISH ROAD. AND SEE, THERE'S A **CHURCH** CLOSE BY!

NOW THERE'LL BE **NO EXCUSE** NOT TO GO!

MANA–WHA?

TURN HERE, CLINT! THIS ONE.

I KNOW, I KNOW.

CAN WE GO FOR A **SWIM** IN THAT **LAKE**?

IT'S A SEWAGE TREATMENT PLANT.

OH.

THEY SAY WE WON'T **SMELL** IT.

SNIF

IT'S **TRUE**. I CAN'T SMELL A **THING**.

GRADE FOUR

SEPTEMBER, 1974

GONNA HAVE TO BUILD A **BIGGER DECK**.

OUGHTA GET SOME CUSHION FLOORING. GONNA HAVE TO **WALLPAPER** TOO.

JESUS CHRIST ALMIGHTY!

WE'RE NOT EVEN **UNPACKED** YET!

TONIGHT IS YOUR FIRST **BROWNIE** MEETING!

DO I **HAVE** TO?

YOU HAVE TO TRY TO MAKE **FRIENDS**.

I TRIED TO SKIP ROPE AT SCHOOL YESTERDAY, BUT I JUST **TRIPPED**.

YOU PROBABLY **GAVE UP** AS SOON AS YOU STARTED.

YOU NEVER **TRUST** ME.

TRUST ISN'T GIVEN, IT'S **EARNED**.

THEY **LAUGHED** AT ME!

JOIN THE **CLUB**.

SEPTEMBER, 1974

OKAY, TEAMS! FORM TWO LINES, WE'RE GOING TO THE **FIELD!**

TIM.

MICHELLE.

DAWN.

GAHHFFF!

WHY'D YOU **DO** THAT?!

I... I REALLY DON'T KNOW WHY I... I'M **SORRY,** I...

ALRIGHT KIDS. **DODGEBALL!** THE MOST FUN YOU'LL HAVE **ALL YEAR!**

SO, HOW WAS **SCHOOL?**

I **HATE** SCHOOL. EVERYONE IS **MEAN**.

YOU SHOULD BE **GRATEFUL** TO GET AN EDUCATION.

BUT IT'S **GYM**. I HATE IT! THEY PICKED ME **LAST** FOR THE TEAM AND THEN WE HAD TO PLAY **DODGEBALL** AND IT WAS **AWFUL!**

WELL, WITH **THAT** HATEFUL ATTITUDE... I DON'T KNOW WHERE YOU GET THAT **MEAN STREAK!**

...AND JACK LEBLANC **PUNCHED** ME RIGHT IN THE **STOMACH!**

YOU'VE GOT TO TAKE THE **BULL** BY THE **HORNS!**

NOBODY EVER GOT ANYWHERE BY BEING A **CRYBABY!**

WHERE ARE **YOU** GOING? YOU JUST GOT HERE! I THOUGHT WE COULD SIT DOWN LIKE A **FAMILY**...

BIG FEED GOING OUT TO THE **LEGION** TONIGHT.

THEN YOU'LL BE STAYING ALL **NIGHT.** SHOULD HAVE KNOWN...

AH, BITE ME **ARMPIT**.

GODDAMNED **DEN OF INEQUITY**, THAT.

YOU HAVEN'T **TOUCHED** YOUR PLATE.

I DON'T **LIKE IT.**

WHAT DID YOU DO, RUIN YOUR SUPPER EATING **CANDY?**

NO! I HATE CANDY AND I **HATE** SCALLOPS!

HATE SCALLOPS!

DO YOU KNOW HOW **LUCKY** YOU ARE? YOU'RE GOING TO EAT **EVERY LAST ONE** OF THOSE SCALLOPS!

OH HONEY. I'M **SO SORRY.** FROM NOW ON I PROMISE I'LL **BELIEVE YOU.**

88

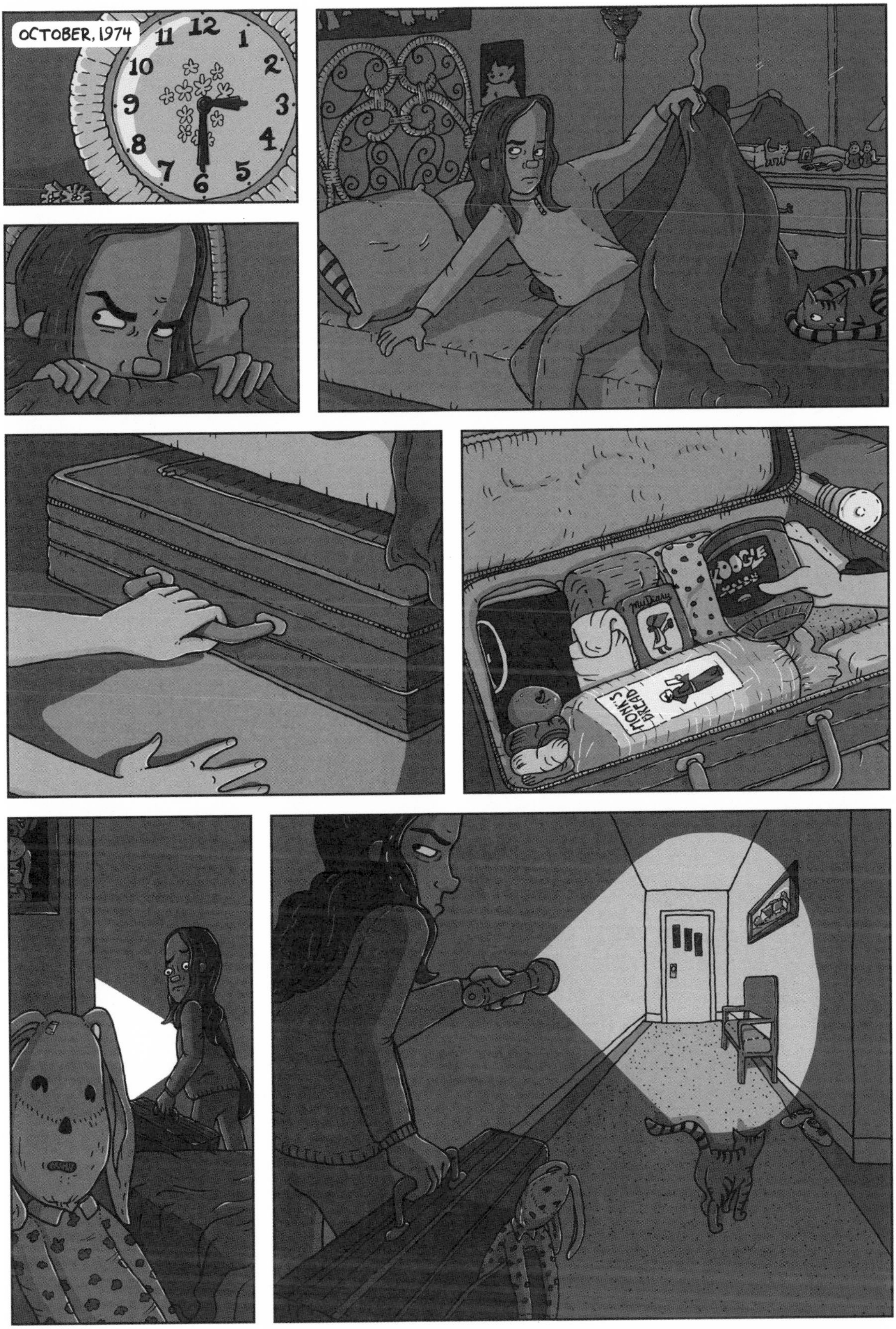
OCTOBER, 1974
My Diary
KOOGLE

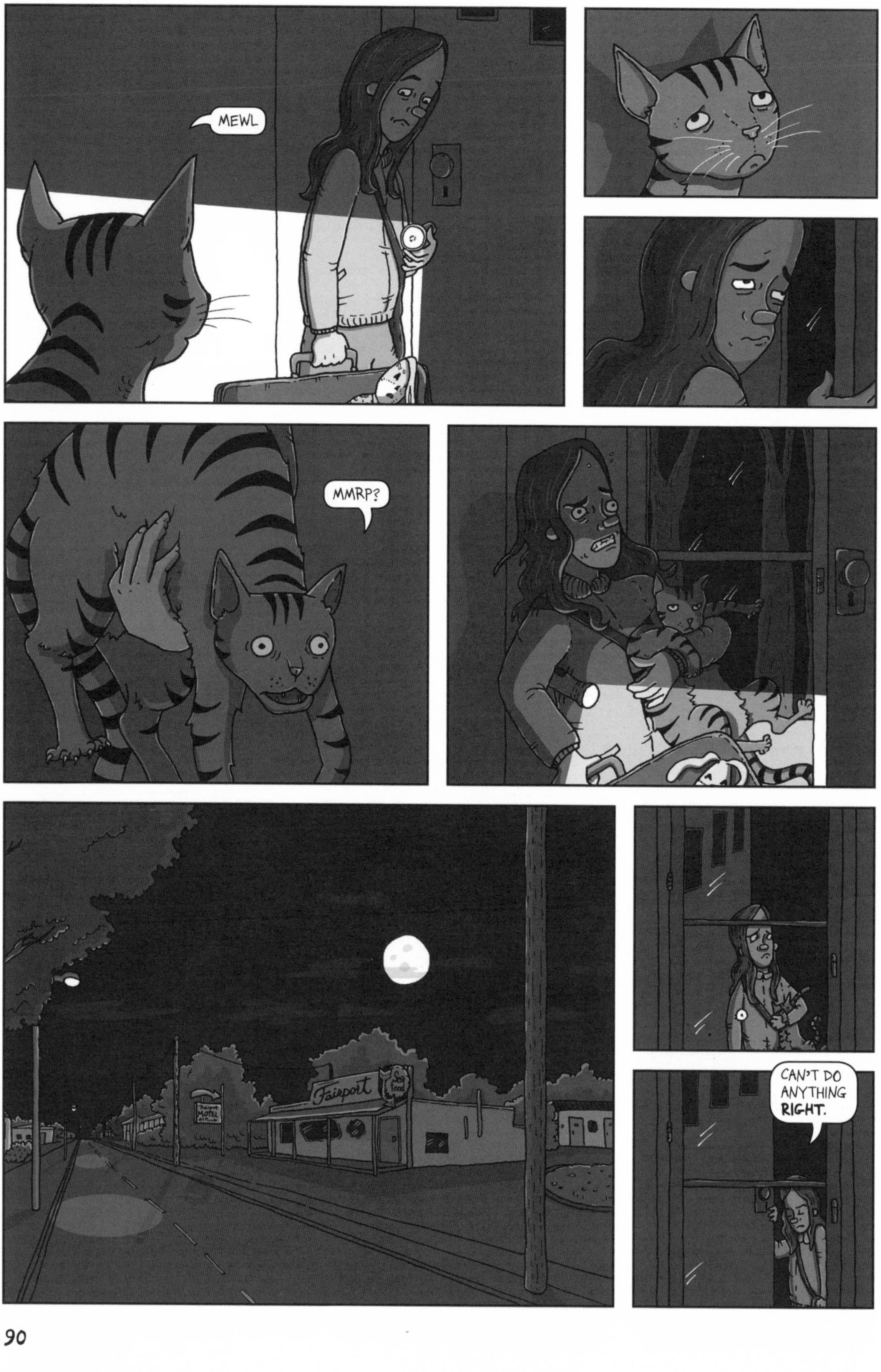
MEWL
MMRP?
Fairport
Sea food
CAN'T DO ANYTHING **RIGHT.**

NOVEMBER, 1974

RESIST NOT EVIL: BUT WHOSOEVER SHALL SMITE THEE ON THY RIGHT CHEEK, TURN TO HIM THE **OTHER** ALSO.

PAY ATTENTION.

ABOUT TIME YOU STARTED TO **LEARN** ABOUT THE **LORD.**

AND IF ANY MAN WILL SUE THEE AT THY LAW AND TAKE AWAY THY COAT, LET HIM HAVE THY CLOAK ALSO.

BUT I SAY UNTO YOU, **LOVE** YOUR **ENEMIES...**

BLESS THEM THAT **CURSE YOU...**

IKOFLDGH FWIUHL FOFMBLL...

MURMURMURURRRRBBBLLMMM...

THAT'S MORE LIKE IT.

BE YE THEREFORE **PERFECT,** EVEN AS YOUR FATHER IN HEAVEN IS PERFECT.

December, 1974

OPEN **ANOTHER** ONE!

BUT MOM, THERE WON'T BE ANY LEFT FOR **TOMORROW**!

OH COME ON. YOU'LL STILL HAVE YOUR **SOCK**! CLINT, **YOU** OPEN ONE.

JESUS CHRIST ALMIGHTY!

PASS HIM THAT **LITTLE** ONE.

WHAT THE HELL IS **THIS**?

IT'S A NOSE WARMER.

HAHAHA!

ALRIGHT, TIME TO HIT THE **SACK**.

WE HAVE TO MAKE THAT SAUCE TOMORROW BEFORE YOUR **SISTERS** SHOW UP.

DAMN RIGHT! WE'RE GONNA MAKE IT **EXTRA HOT** THIS YEAR!

OPEN THAT **LAST** GIFT!

A **TAPE RECORDER**! WOW! THANKS, MOM!

NOW DON'T SAY I NEVER DO ANYTHING FOR YOU!

NOW LET'S SEE IF THERE'S A **LATE MOVIE** ON.

YEAH!

JANUARY, 1975

AND I'M OUT.

JAYZ–US! YOU FILTHY ROTTEN SON OF A BITCH.

CLINTON, YOU'RE A DIRTY PLAYER!

LOOK WHAT I GOT STUCK WITH! YA BUGGERS! TEN! TWENTY! FORTY! EVERY KING IN THE DECK! ARGH!

CHRISTERS! THE LOTTA YA!

DON'T TELL ME YOU'VE BEEN TAPING US!

YOU JEEZLY DEVIL!

JAYZUS, JOSEPH AND MARY! DINGLEDORF! GODDAMN SONUVABITCH! JESUS H CHRIST!

93

JANUARY, 1975

SO **HELGA** SAID,

'WHY **SHOULD** I GIVE YOU YOUR MONEY BACK? YOU ATE EVERY LAST **GODDAMN PIECE** OF THAT SEAFOOD DINNER!'

HEH

HEH. SHE'S A **HOT DUCK**, THAT ONE.

MOM, ER... WHAT DOES **FUCK** MEAN, ANYWAY?

WHERE DID YOU HEAR **THAT**?!

I DON'T **EVER** WANT TO HEAR YOU USE THAT WORD **AGAIN!**

I'M NOT **USING** IT, I JUST WANT TO KNOW WHAT IT **MEANS**.

IT'S A VERY **BAD** WORD.

BUT WHAT DOES IT **MEAN?**

YOU DON'T NEED TO KNOW THAT.

HOT CHICKEN SAND 1.00
HAMBURGER .75
HOT DOG .30
FRIES LG.50 SM.30
LIVER+ONIONS 1.25
FRIED BALONEY .50

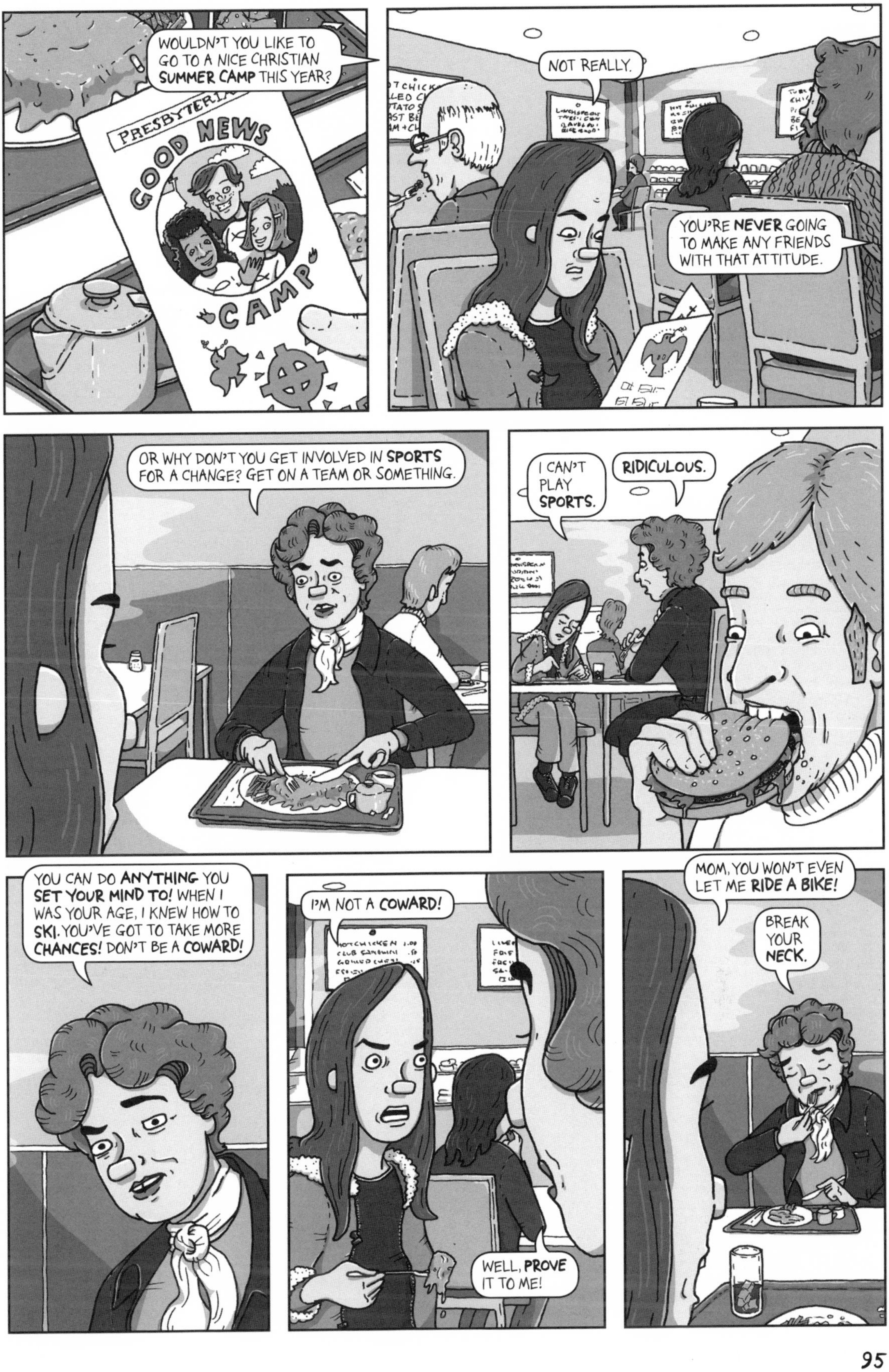
WOULDN'T YOU LIKE TO GO TO A NICE CHRISTIAN SUMMER CAMP THIS YEAR?
PRESBYTERIA
GOOD NEWS
CAMP
NOT REALLY.
YOU'RE NEVER GOING TO MAKE ANY FRIENDS WITH THAT ATTITUDE.
OR WHY DON'T YOU GET INVOLVED IN SPORTS FOR A CHANGE? GET ON A TEAM OR SOMETHING.
I CAN'T PLAY SPORTS.
RIDICULOUS.
YOU CAN DO ANYTHING YOU SET YOUR MIND TO! WHEN I WAS YOUR AGE, I KNEW HOW TO SKI. YOU'VE GOT TO TAKE MORE CHANCES! DON'T BE A COWARD!
I'M NOT A COWARD!
WELL, PROVE IT TO ME!
MOM, YOU WON'T EVEN LET ME RIDE A BIKE!
BREAK YOUR NECK.

FEBRUARY, 1975

THIS CRUST'LL MAKE IT GO **REALLY** FAST!

WOOOO!!!

AHHH!!

UH OH.

ABANDON SHIP!

UNF.

FUUUCK...

MARCH, 1975

MY CLASS IS PUTTING ON A PLAY AND I'M **IN IT!**

I'LL BE **DAMNED!** IS IT THE **LEAD?**

SHOULDA **KNOWN.**

WHAT'S THE PLAY?

NO...

IT'S **CINDERELLA** BUT IT'S SPACE-AGE.

WE'LL HAVE TO MAKE YOU A **COSTUME!** GO TELL YOUR **FATHER.**

GUESS WHAT, DAD?

DON'T TELL ME THERE'S ANOTHER **JEEZLY** HOCKEY GAME ON AGAIN TONIGHT!

JESUS CHRIST ALMIGHTY! CAN'T A GUY GET ANY **PEACE** AROUND HERE?

I'VE GOT A PART IN A **PLAY!**

MOVE, WILL YA?

I DON'T SUPPOSE YOU TRIED OUT FOR THE **BASKETBALL** TEAM, EH?

WELL... NO...

LEMME KNOW WHEN YOU JOIN A **TEAM.**

OOH, FIGHT! **FIGHT!**

MARCH, 1975

WHAT DID YOU DO WITH THE GLUE?

HUH?

IT'S THE FINAL DAY FOR MY **MATCH THE TWINS** CONTEST!

I DIDN'T DO ANYTHING WITH IT.

DON'T **LIE** TO ME, USE YOUR **HEAD**! WHERE DID YOU PUT IT?

I'M **NOT** LYING!

WHY DO YOU WANT TO **RUIN THIS** FOR ME?

I DIDN'T TAKE THE GLUE!

JESUS CHRIST ALMIGHTY! YOU LOOKIN' FOR THE **GLUE**, IT'S DOWN ON MY WORKBENCH.

SEE!

YOU SAID YOU'D **BELIEVE** ME FROM NOW ON!

OKAY, OKAY. I'M **SORRY**. I WAS WRONG. NOW GO GET ME THE GLUE.

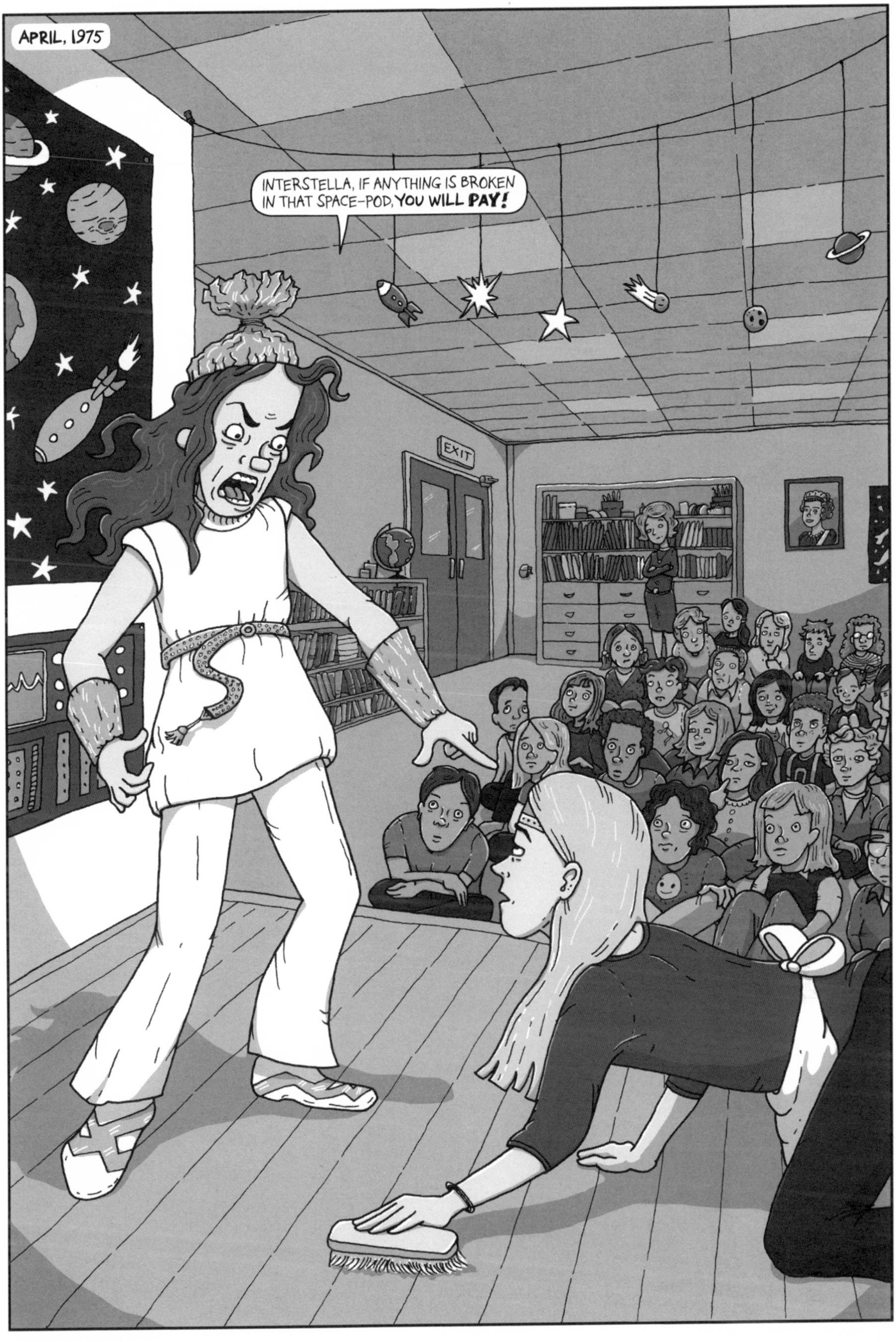
APRIL, 1975
INTERSTELLA, IF ANYTHING IS BROKEN IN THAT SPACE-POD, **YOU WILL PAY!**
EXIT

MAY, 1975

HEY, YOU WERE RIGHT FUNNY IN THAT **PLAY!**

OH UH...THANKS.

I'M GOIN' TO **SKIP ROPE** WITH STEPHANIE AND JESSICA. WANNA COME?

UM...

I CAN'T... I MEAN... I'M REALLY **BAD** AT IT.

SURE YOU CAN, IT'S **EASY.** COME ON, I'LL **SHOW** YOU!

OKAY!

AYY-YYY!

JUNE, 1975

DOESN'T THE WAX **BURN**?

AT FIRST YES, BUT YOU JUST GO A LITTLE AT A TIME... **TRY** IT.

THIS MAKES YOUR **ARTHRITIS** BETTER?

FOR A LITTLE WHILE.

WALLPAPERING THIS DAMN KITCHEN JUST ABOUT **KILLED** ME. DON'T KNOW **WHEN** I'LL GET AROUND TO YOUR ROOM.

CAN'T WE JUST PAINT IT **BLACK**?

THAT'S THE MOST RIDICULOUS THING ON THE FACE OF THE **EARTH**. BLACK. IN A LITTLE GIRL'S ROOM. **IMAGINE**.

IS IT OKAY IF I HAVE **PAM** OVER?

YOU HAVE A LOT OF **HOUSEWORK** TO DO.

AFTER THAT?

I DON'T KNOW IF I **LIKE** THAT PAM.

WHY?! SHE'S SO NICE!

SHE'S A BIT OF A SHOW-OFF WITH ALL THAT **AY-YY-YY**. PROBABLY GOING TO BE A **BAD INFLUENCE**.

SHE JUST LIKES **THE FONZ**.

I **HATE** THAT **FONZIE**.

MOM, YOU **WANTED** ME TO HAVE FRIENDS!

JULY, 1975

YOU'RE GETTING THE **HANG** OF IT!

CAN I RIDE IT OVER TO PAM'S HOUSE?

NO. GET YOURSELF **KILLED.**

IT'S PERFECT **HERE!** SUNDAY AFTERNOON, EVERYTHING'S **CLOSED**...

WELL, CAN I RIDE IT BACK HOME? IT'S SO **CLOSE!**

NO. IN A FEW MONTHS YOU SHOULD BE READY FOR THE ROAD.

IN A FEW MONTHS IT'LL BE **WINTER.**

ALL THE **OTHER** KIDS...

YOU'RE NOT ALL THE OTHER KIDS. YOU'RE MY **DAUGHTER.**

AUGUST, 1975

YOUR BROTHER IS AS **HANDSOME** AS THE **DAY** THAT I MARRIED HIM!

HEH HEH.

RUNS IN THE FAMILY I GUESS!

OH, YOU ATE YOUR SOUP **ALL UP!** YOU'RE GOING TO GROW UP SO **BIG** AND **STRONG!**

RRRRR

LOBSTER NEWBURG FOR **YOU**, MADAM.

I COULDN'T RESIST.

OOOOH! LOOKIT THAT!

AND IF YOU EAT **THIS** ALL UP, YOU CAN HAVE **DESSERT!**

WHY DO YOU HAVE TO HAVE THAT **HATEFUL LOOK** ON YOUR FACE?

THAT WAITER...

HE'S A BIT MUCH, ISN'T HE?

HE'S TREATING ME LIKE A **BABY**.

LET'S TRY ONE OF THOSE **HARVEY WALLBANGERS.**

OOOH, YES!

AND WOULD YOU LIKE A **SHIRLEY TEMPLE**? OR A NICE, BIG GLASS OF **MILK**?

TEA, PLEASE.

TEA!

THAT'S WHAT SHE ASKED FOR.

ONLY CHILDREN.

GRADE FIVE

SEPTEMBER, 1975

I CAN'T BELIEVE MOM LET ME COME TO THIS **SHOW!**

SHRIEK!

AHHH!

HEY **MARY ANNE,** CAN WE GO GET SOMETHING TO EAT?

AFTER **THAT** MOVIE? I DON' **KNOW...**

LET'S GO TO **KENTUCKY FRIED!**

WE CAN'T GO THERE! YOUR FATHER'D **PUT THE BOOTS TO ME!**

OCTOBER, 1975

I HOPE EVERYBODY LIKES **FRIED CHICKEN!**

AWRIGHT!

I DO!

YEAH!

TODAY, DAWN'S FATHER HAS BROUGHT US A **SPECIAL LUNCH TREAT.**

GET IT WHILE IT'S **HOT!**

YUMMY! YOUR DAD IS THE **BEST!** YOU'RE SO **LUCKY!**

HE'S NOT **QUITE** LIKE THAT AT HOME...

ENOUGH **POP** FOR EVERYONE!

HE SURE **SEEMS** PRETTY GREAT.

AYY-YYY!

LOOKIT! I'M JAWS!

JAWS IS MY FAVOURITE!

ME TOO! I LOVE SHARKS!

ME TOO! THE SHARK IS VERY SCARY! I SAW IT TWICE!

MY BROTHER IS SCARED TO TAKE A BATH!

YEAH!

MAYBE WE SHOULD FORM A CLUB!

SO ISN'T THIS THE SAME THING AS THE COLONEL?

NO IT'S NOT THE SAME THING!

IT'S ONLY THE BEST CHICKEN YOU'LL EVER EAT!

NOVEMBER, 1975

YOUR DAUGHTER TAUGHT HERSELF HOW TO PLAY **YELLOW BIRD** TODAY. YOU OUGHTA HEAR HER!

I'LL NEED THE CAR TOMORROW...

...I HAVE AN APPOINTMENT WITH THE **SPECIALIST.**

CLINTON?

JESUS CHRIST ALMIGHTY.

DOESN'T **ANYTHING** IN THIS FAMILY **MATTER** TO YOU?

OBITUARIES

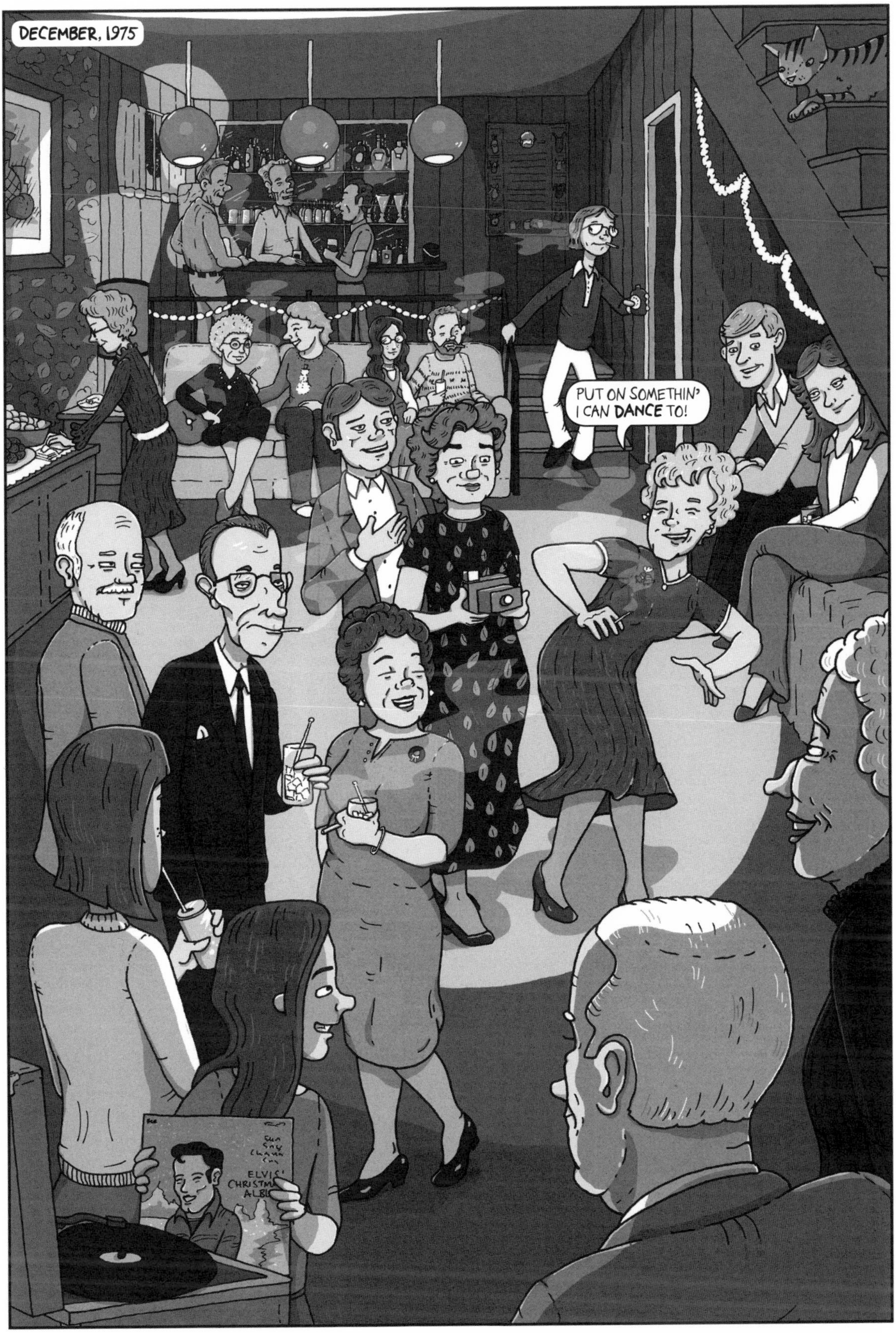
DECEMBER, 1975
PUT ON SOMETHIN' I CAN **DANCE** TO!

JANUARY, 1976

THIS IS YOUR **MOTHER'S** SIGNATURE, IS IT?

YES...

YOUR MOTHER DIDN'T TYPE THIS. **NOR** DID SHE SIGN IT.

YOU'RE **STILL** GOING TO **LIE!** YOU'RE ONLY MAKING IT **WORSE** ON YOURSELF, YOU KNOW!

I'M SORRY! I'M SORRY! I WON'T DO IT **AGAIN!**

ARE YOU AWARE THAT FORGERY IS **ILLEGAL?**

TAKE THIS. YOUR MOTHER IS WAITING TO SEE IT.

Dawn must stay inside at lunc htime and recess because she has a cold.

Since rely,

Phyllis Bo

YOU EXPECTED THEM TO **BELIEVE** THIS MESS?

MY **OWN** DAUGHTER! A **FORGER!**

I'M SORRY.

DAMN RIGHT YOU'RE SORRY! AFTER ALL WE DO FOR YOU, **THIS** IS HOW YOU REPAY US?

I JUST WANTED TO STAY IN AT LUNCHTIME.

WHY? WHAT KID DOESN'T WANT TO **GO** OUTSIDE?

WELL... THERE'S THIS BOY...

WHAT BOY?

HIS NAME IS **DANIEL** AND HE HAS TO STAY INSIDE... HE'S GOT ASTHMA OR SOMETHING...

YOU CAN **PICK** 'EM.

I will not commit forgery. Forgery is a crime.

FILL OUT **EVERY PAGE** OF THIS BOOK WITH THOSE LINES. AND DON'T THINK THAT'S ALL THAT'S COMING TO YOU.

AND YOU'RE TOO YOUNG FOR **BOYS!** BOYS ONLY WANT **ONE THING!** YOU SHOULD **NEVER** ENCOURAGE THEM!

FEBRUARY, 1976

OW! THAT **HURT!**

'OW THAT HURT.'

SCARED?

BECAUSE I **WANT** TO.

WHY ARE YOU **DOING THIS?!**

114

HEH. KIDS LOVE **SNOW!**

STOP! **STOP!**

THAT'S MY **HOUSE** AND MY **PARENTS** ARE HOME SO YOU BETTER GO AWAY OR YOU'LL BE **SORRY!!**

WHY IS EVERYONE SO **MEAN?**

I WAS **WORRIED SICK!** WHERE **WERE** YOU?

PLAYING IN THE **SNOW?** WITH **BOYS?** YOU PROMISED ME YOU WOULD WALK **STRAIGHT HOME** AFTER SCHOOL!

AND WHERE'S YOUR **HAT?**

I LOST IT.

CAN'T I **TRUST** YOU WITH ANYTHING?

MARCH, 1976

I DREW TYRANNO-SAURUS 'CUZ HE'S THE MOST **FEROCIOUS.**

RAR!

Tyrannosaurus Rex

RAR!

MY DINO IS TRICERATOPS. HE CAN **PIERCE THE HIDES** OF HIS ENEMIES.

Triceratops

MINE'S STEGOSAURUS BECAUSE HE CAN **PROTECT HIMSELF.**

ONLY YOU

Stegosaurus

DINOSHARK CLUB

HEY **NERDS!**

BLACK AT

IT'S LUNCHTIME! MIGHT BE THE **LAST SNOW** OF THE YEAR! **LET'S GO!**

I CAN'T.

SIX MILLION DOLLAR MAN

HEH HEH!

SNICKER.

AN APPLE A DAY

KEEPS DOCTOR

DINOSHARK

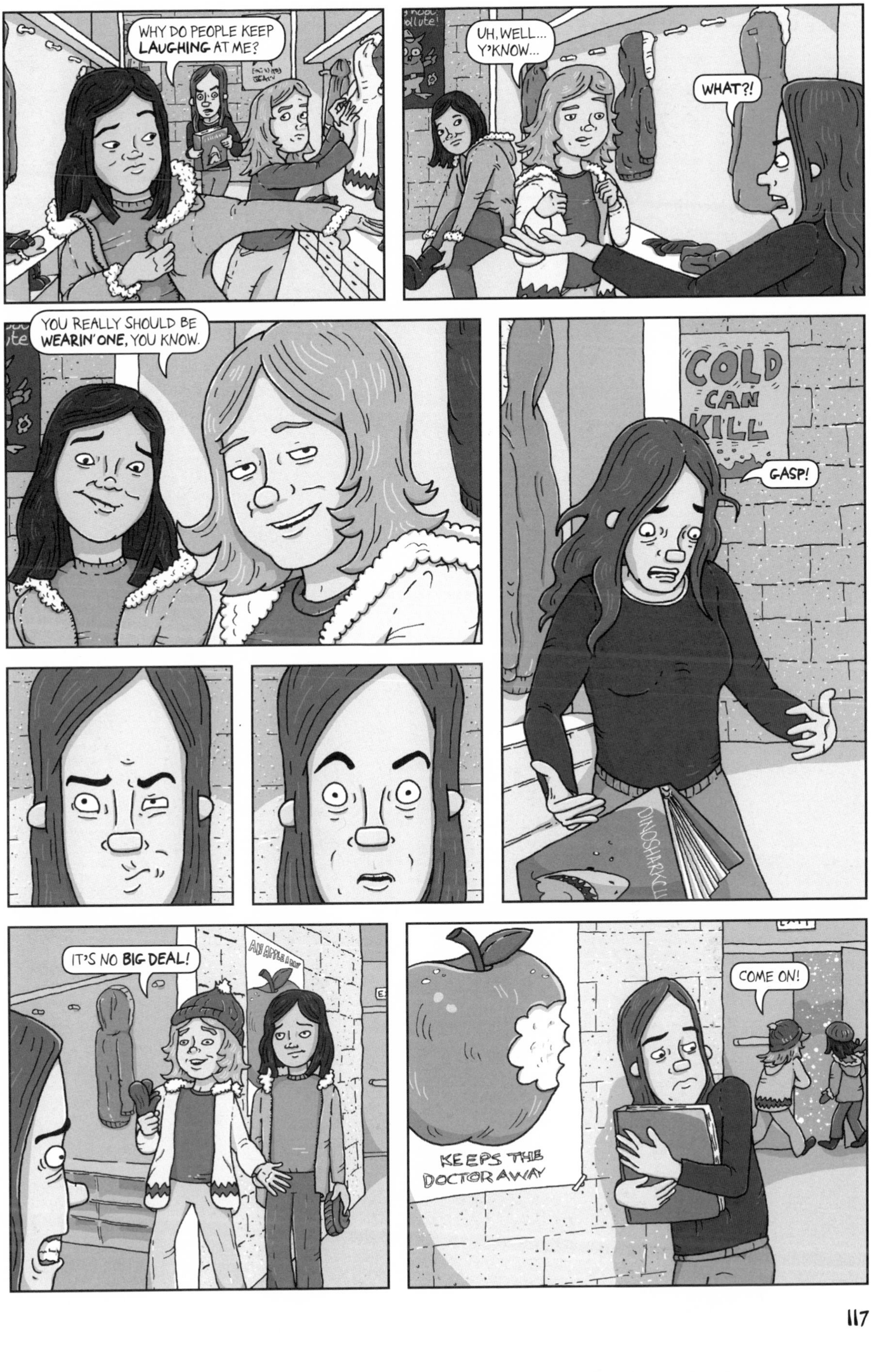
WHY DO PEOPLE KEEP **LAUGHING** AT ME?
UH, WELL... Y'KNOW...
WHAT?!
YOU REALLY SHOULD BE **WEARIN' ONE,** YOU KNOW.
COLD CAN KILL
GASP!
IT'S NO **BIG DEAL!**
KEEPS THE DOCTOR AWAY
COME ON!

APRIL, 1976

TRY THIS ONE. STOP SLOUCHING.

AGGH! MOM! THIS ONE'S GOOD ENOUGH.

IT DOESN'T FIT RIGHT. IT'S TOO BIG AROUND THE **RIBCAGE**, SEE?

MO-O-OM!

HERE'S THE BOX. SHE'LL JUST WEAR THE **BRA** HOME.

GIRLS

fitting rooms

CAN I GO TO THE **TOY** DEPARTMENT NOW?

DON'T BE TOO LONG. I'M GOING TO LOOK AT **PATTERNS**.

HELLOOOO THERE!

GASP!

SLIME

BAHAHAHA!

THAT WAS **QUICK!** GETTING A BIT TOO **OLD** FOR TOYS NOW, EH?

MAY, 1976

HEY, DON'T YOU **LIVE** NEAR ME?

YOU HAVE A **PUG**, RIGHT?

YEAH. **PUGGLES!**

HE'S CUTE.

HEY, WANNA CHECK OUT OUR COOL **SECRET SPOT?**

LOOKIT **VINNIE BARBARINO.** HE'S **RIGHT CUTE,** EH?

HEY, WHAT'S IN **HERE?**

NONE OF YOUR **BUSINESS,** PUG–FACE!

YEAH! GO AWAY, **PUG–FACE!** THIS IS **OUR** SPOT!

DON'T CALL ME THAT! YOU TAKE THAT **BACK!**

PUG–FACE! PUG–FACE!

I'M GONNA **TELL** ON **ALL OF YOU!**

I HOPE WE DON'T GET IN **TROUBLE** FOR THAT.

THESE ARE THE GIRLS WHO CALLED YOU BY THAT NAME?

MR. RIB

YES. HER AND **HER**.

BUT... WHERE'S **CHARLOTTE**? I DIDN'T EVEN...

IT'S NOT YOUR **TURN** TO **SPEAK**.

YOU SHOULD BE **ASHAMED** OF YOURSELF.

A GOOD STUDENT LIKE YOU! I DO **NOT** TOLERATE **BULLIES**.

JENNIE HERE HAS A CLEAN RECORD, AND SHE'S **CLEARLY** SORRY FOR WHAT SHE'S DONE.

PRINCIPAL'S OFFICE

YES! I'M **SORRY**! SOB! SOB!

DAWN, **APOLOGIZE** TO SUE.

SORRY.

IF I SEE YOU IN MY OFFICE AGAIN NEXT YEAR, IT'S THE **STRAP**.

121

CRICK! SKRAK! CRITCH!

CRAWK CRAWK!

I WAS **FRAMED**!

THE OTHER GIRLS DID IT BUT I **DIDN'T**! I'M NOT A **BULLY**!

DID YOU **PLAY ALONG** WITH IT?

DID YOU **STAND UP** FOR THAT GIRL?

NO... I GUESS I DIDN'T... TRY...

DON'T BE A **COWARD**!

SHE POINTED **RIGHT AT ME** AND SAID **I DID IT**! THE MEANEST GIRL WASN'T EVEN **SENT** TO THE PRINCIPAL'S OFFICE!

IT'S NOT FAIR!!

YOU'RE SO ANGRY, IT **MUST** BE THE TRUTH.

THAT OPENS 'ER UP!

JUNE, 1976

THEY'RE NOT SERVING **CONEY ISLAND SAUCE** ANYMORE.

AW! WHAT ELSE IS GOING TO **CHANGE?!**

I CAN'T WAIT TO VISIT **JACKIE!** I WISH IT WAS AUGUST ALREADY!

NEVER WISH YOUR **LIFE** AWAY, HON.

SO YOU DO REMEMBER JACKIE. OPINIONATED. AQUARIUS. JUST LIKE **ME**. USED TO BE A **DANCER**, YOU KNOW.

NOW SHE'S INTO **WOMEN'S LIB**. I WISH **YOU** LIKED TO **DANCE**.

I LIKE **ACTING**. THAT WAS FUN.

THE OTHER KIDS SAID I WAS **GOOD!**

OH, NO...

ACTORS ARE **ALWAYS** OUT OF WORK...UNLESS YOU'RE **FAMOUS**, AND WHO WANTS **THAT**? CAN'T MAKE A MOVE WITHOUT PEOPLE JUDGING EVERYTHING YOU DO!

YOU **DON'T** WANT TO BE AN ACTOR.

NO. NO, I GUESS NOT.

HITCH YOUR **WAGON** TO A **STAR!** WHY AIM FOR **THAT** WHEN YOU CAN BE **ANYTHING** YOU WANT TO BE?

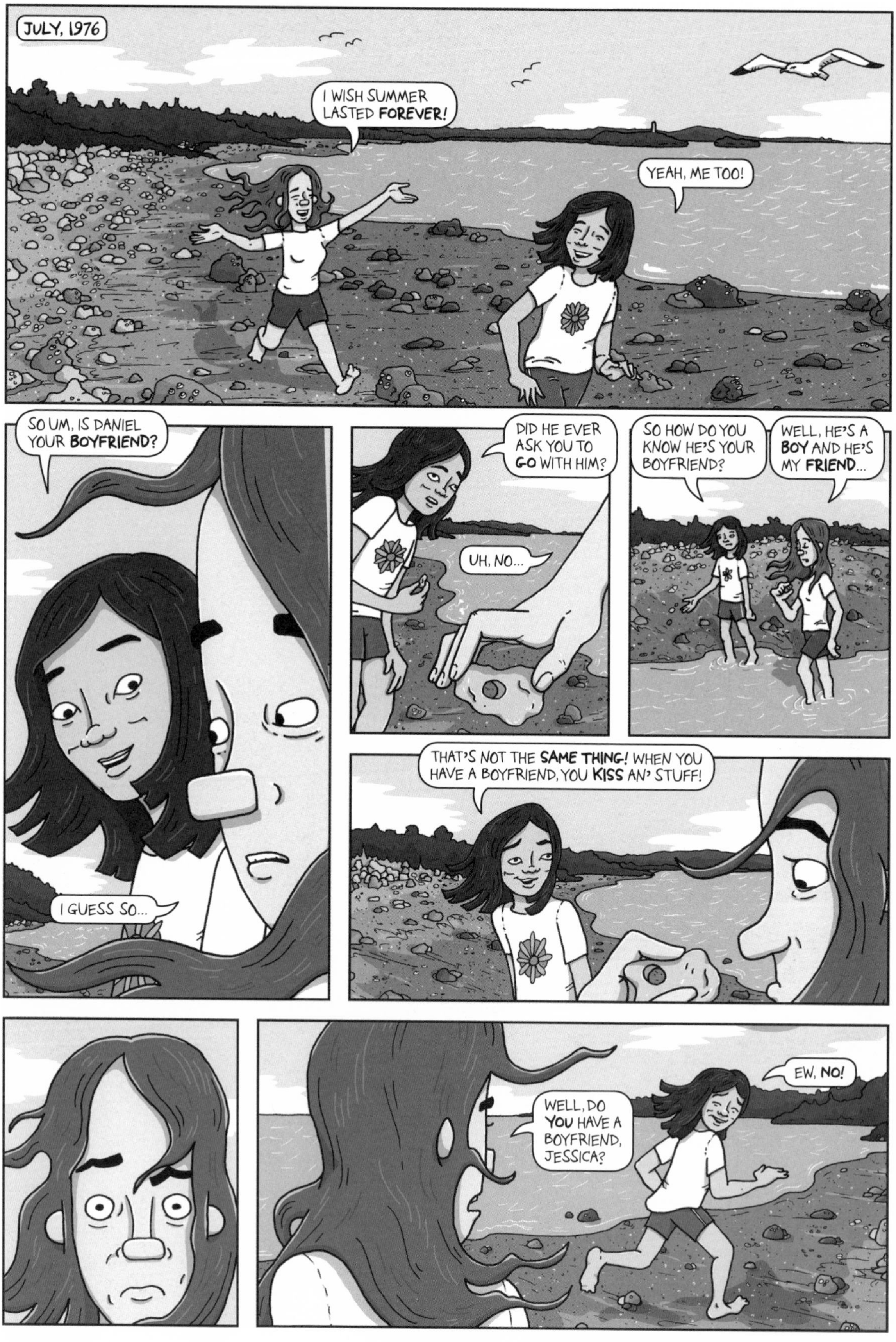
JULY, 1976
I WISH SUMMER LASTED FOREVER!
YEAH, ME TOO!
SO UM, IS DANIEL YOUR BOYFRIEND?
I GUESS SO...
DID HE EVER ASK YOU TO GO WITH HIM?
UH, NO...
SO HOW DO YOU KNOW HE'S YOUR BOYFRIEND?
WELL, HE'S A BOY AND HE'S MY FRIEND...
THAT'S NOT THE SAME THING! WHEN YOU HAVE A BOYFRIEND, YOU KISS AN' STUFF!
WELL, DO YOU HAVE A BOYFRIEND, JESSICA?
EW, NO!

JULY, 1976

ALRIGHT, YOU CAN **COME OUT** NOW.

CAN'T THEY SEE THE **BIG LUMP** IN THE BACK SEAT?

MY LEGS ARE **WAY** TOO LONG FOR THAT!

THEY'D NEVER SUSPECT TWO **OLD FOGIES** LIKE US TO BE **SMUGGLING** PEOPLE IN.

SPEAK FOR **YOURSELF!**

AND AN ORDER OF **ONION RINGS!** THEY'RE SOME **JEEZLY GOOD!**

Let's All Go To The L

125

DO YOU HAVE A **BOYFRIEND**?

YEAH! DOUG!

WHAT DO YOU GUYS DO?

OH, YOU KNOW. WE GO TO PARTIES, OR MCDONALD'S OR SOMEWHERES LIKE THAT.

DO YOU... LIKE... UM

KISS 'N' STUFF?

THAT'S **NONE OF YOUR BUSINESS**! NOW COME ON, THE SHOW'S STARTING.

HEY MARY ANNE, DO YOU BELIEVE IN **ASTROLOGY**?

ALLS I KNOW IS I'M A CANCER.

I'M A **LIBRA** AND THE BOOK SAID I NEED A **BOYFRIEND**.

DO YOU **GOT** ONE?

NO.

I GUESS YOU DON'T **NEED** ONE, THEN.

YOUNG FRANKENSTEIN

AUGUST, 1976

IT'S ABOUT TIME TO GRAB A BITE, SYB.

YOU SAID IT! DAWN, WE'RE GONNA CALL IT A **DAY**.

Your *Dreaming* MIND

BUT THERE'S STILL A **WHOLE** OTHER SECTION!

NEXT **TIME** WE VISIT **JACKIE**.

SOUNDLESS CHAMBER

AW BUT... CAN'T I AT **LEAST** GO IN **THERE**?

I HAVE TO SIT DOWN, MY **FEET** ARE **KILLING** ME.

I CAN GO BY **MYSELF**! **JEEZ** MOM!

UNC

WELL, HURRY UP AND BE **CAREFUL**. YOU CAN'T TRUST **ANYBODY**, YOU KNOW!

I KNOW, I KNOW.

HEE HEE HEE HEE!

IT'S NOT REALLY **THAT** SOUNDLESS.

WHERE ARE YOU GOING? HMM?

ALL ALONE EH? SCARED? HUH?

YOU SHOULD BE 'CUZ NO-ONE CAN HEAR YOU!

C'MON, MAN, LET HER GO, SOMEONE'S COMING.

BUH-BYE!

THAT WAS QUICK.

CAN WE GO NOW?

A MINUTE AGO YOU WANTED TO STAY.

WELL I WANT TO GO NOW!

PERCEPTION

MIND'S EYE

SPOILED ROTTEN.

ONLY CHILDREN.

MEMORY

128

GRADE SIX

SEPTEMBER, 1976

...WELL YOU CAME AND YOU GAVE WITHOUT TAKIN'...

WHAT ARE YOU **UP TO** IN HERE?

MOM! I WAS **TAPING** THAT SONG!

YOU KNOW I DON'T LIKE **CLOSED DOORS.**

A CLOSED DOOR MEANS YOU'RE **UP TO SOMETHING** YOU DON'T WANT ME TO SEE.

I JUST LIKE A LITTLE **PRIVACY.**

NOW WHAT DO **YOU** NEED PRIVACY FOR?

WHO'S THAT NOW? IS THAT THAT **REPROBATE** FROM THAT **FRANKENSTEIN** MOVIE?

MOM. IT'S **GENE WILDER.**

I SHOULD **NEVER** HAVE TAKEN YOU TO THAT SHOW. **SEX, SEX, SEX,** THAT'S **ALL** THEY CAN **THINK** ABOUT THESE DAYS...

131

MO-O-OM!

ANYWAY, UH... I WANTED TO **TALK** TO YOU...

ABOUT...

HAVE THEY TAUGHT YOU ANYTHING YET... ABOUT... ER... THE **CHANGE**... UH, WOMANHOOD...

WELL UM, YOU MEAN... UH, NOT REALLY, A BIT... UM...

WITH ALL THAT DAMN **SEX EDUCATION** IN SCHOOL NOWADAYS...

IT MUSTA **COME UP.**

HERE... READ **THIS.** IF YOU HAVE ANY **QUESTIONS,** ASK ME.

REMEMBER, YOU CAN **TALK** TO ME ABOUT **ANYTHING!**

Your Time of the Month

OCTOBER, 1976

WALTER SAF... GASP!

EXTEND YOUR REACH

HONK HONK!

HAHAHA HAAAA!

BAHAHAHA!

SCHOOL

Give a hoot! Don't Pollute

SCHOOL SPIRI

WHAT'S WRONG?

NOTHING.

I WROTE A STORY FOR THE CLUB!

JAWS MEETS WONDER WOMAN
THE END

DIDN'T REALLY GET THE BOOBS RIGHT.

OCTOBER, 1976

QUICKSAND. HELP.

WHAT ARE YOU SO HAPPY ABOUT?

I'LL WIPE THAT **SMILE** OFF YOUR FACE.

134

DECEMBER, 1976

WHATCHA **DOIN'** DOWN THERE?

WATCHING A **SHOW.**

WE COULD WATCH IT **TOGETHER.**

WE COULD HAVE A NICE CUP OF **TEA** AND SOME OF THOSE **DREAM** SQUARES...

GEEZ MOM! MY FAVOURITE PART IS ON!

WHATEVER I TOUCH TURNS TO SNOW IN MY CLUTCH...

I'M TOO MUCH!

JANUARY, 1977

YOURS IS THE BEST! THE **WINNER** GETS A **CHICKEN SNACK!**

AND MOM SAID YOU CAN COME TO **HOJO'S** WITH US ON MARCH BREAK!

RATS! I WON'T BE ABLE TO GO CUZ?...

MY PARENTS JUST TOLD ME THAT WE'RE **MOVING AWAY** AT THE END OF THE MONTH.

BUT WE CAN BE **PEN PALS!**

GOTTA GO TO **PRACTICE!**

WE CAN **WRITE** TO EACH OTHER **FOREVER!**

WAH WAH! AH HAHAA!

AHHHG!

WHY ARE YOU **DOING THIS** TO ME?!

BAHA!

I DON'T KNOW.

IT MAKES MY **HANDS** FEEL GOOD!

PLEASE STOP!

BAH HAHA! NO WAY!

BWAAAAAAH!!!

GOOD **HEAVENS!** WHAT'S **WRONG?**

TERRY... HE **GRABS** ME!! HE GRABS ME... **HERE!** EVERYONE **LAUGHS!** IT HURTS!

EASY NOW. HE WON'T THINK IT'S SO **FUNNY** AFTER THE **STRAP.**

WOULD YOU LIKE ME TO CALL YOUR **MOTHER** TO COME PICK YOU UP?

GASP! NO!

137

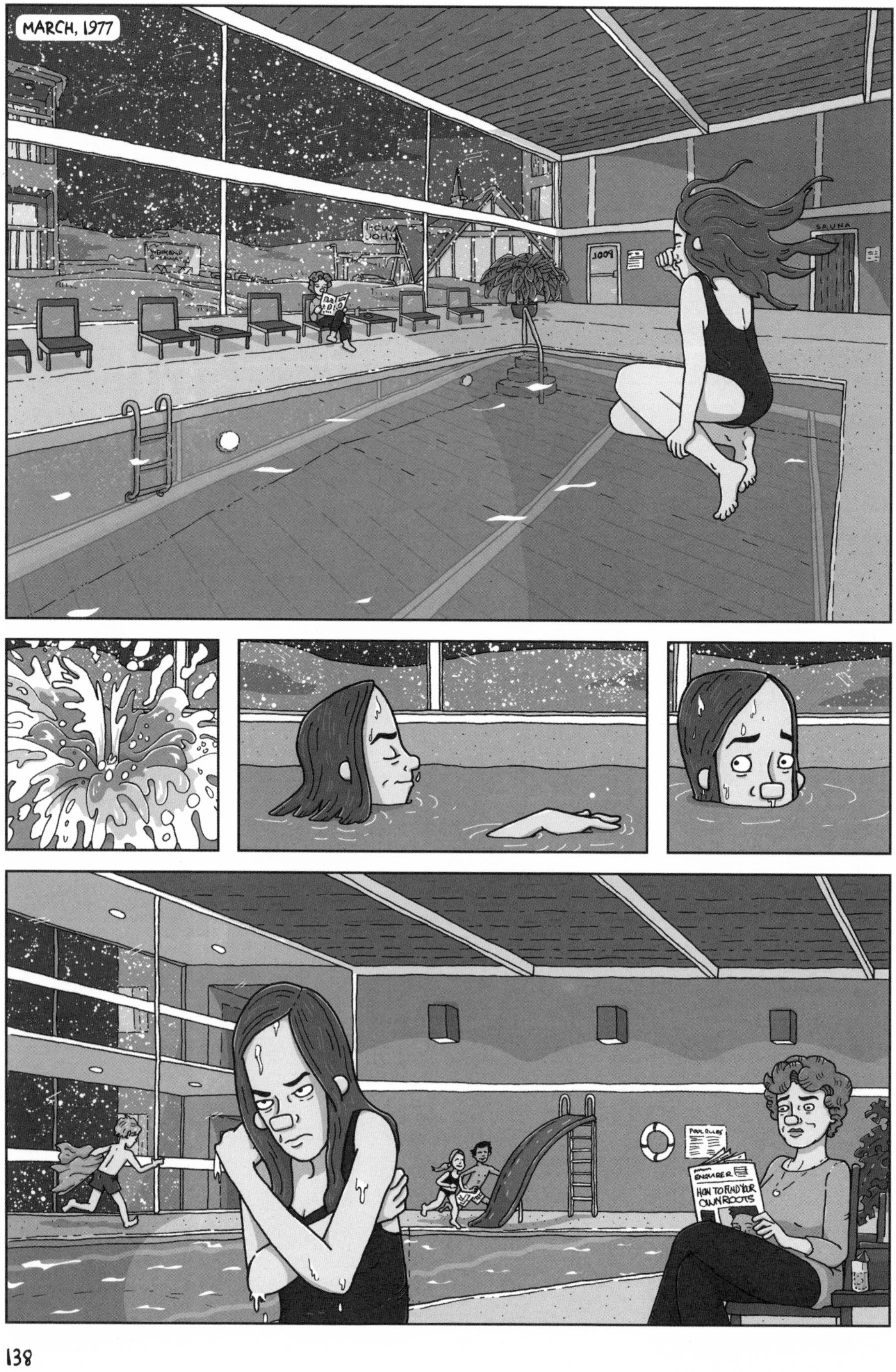
MARCH, 1977
SAUNA
1009
POOL RULES
ENQUIRER
HOW TO FIND YOUR OWN ROOTS

APRIL, 1977

SO THEN HE **RIPPED OFF** HIS **ARM!** TURNS OUT BIGFOOT'S A **ROBOT!** THEN THE **ALIENS** CAPTURED **STEVE!** THEN...

IT SOUNDS **STUPID.**

JEEZ, ARE YOU EVER IN A **BAD MOOD** TODAY!

WOAH. ARE YOU **OKAY?**

URRGH.

I DUNNO. I DON'T **FEEL** GOOD, I HAVE THIS **PAIN**...

MAYBE YOU SHOULD GO TO THE **SICK ROOM.**

PROBABLY GET IN **TROUBLE** FOR THAT.

WHY ARE YOU HOME **EARLY?**

I HAD TO GO TO THE SICK ROOM TODAY.

NOT **AGAIN!**

I WAS SICK... MY GUTS...

I'LL **BET!** SICK OF **MATH!**

MOM, THAT WAS **GRADE TWO!** I MAKE **A's** IN MATH NOW! WHY DON'T YOU **EVER** TRUST ME?!

TRUST ISN'T **GIVEN,** IT'S **EARNED.**

WHAT DO I HAVE TO DO TO **EARN IT?!**

WHAT'RE YOU WASHING?

I GOT MY PERIOD.

OH... DAWN. I'M SORRY. I DIDN'T EVEN THINK... I SHOULD HAVE BELIEVED YOU.

YOU NEVER BELIEVE ME! I'M AFRAID TO TELL YOU ANYTHING! EVERYTHING'S MY FAULT! NOTHING'S EVER GOOD ENOUGH!

OH HONEY. I'M SO PROUD OF YOU.

I ONLY WANT TO BE AS HONEST WITH YOU AS I CAN...

SO THAT YOU CAN BE YOUR BEST... BE PREPARED FOR HOW HARD THE WORLD IS.

IF YOU HAVE A THIN SKIN, YOU GET HURT ALL THE TIME.

I'M RAISING YOU THE BEST WAY I KNOW HOW.

BUT YOU'RE ALWAYS MAD AT ME! I CAN'T DO ANYTHING RIGHT!

141

I NEVER MEAN TO **HURT YOU**. OH, I JUST CAN'T KEEP MY **BIG MOUTH SHUT**. I KNOW, I'M NOT **EASY** TO GET ALONG WITH... BUT I **LOVE YOU** MORE THAN **ANYTHING** IN THE **WORLD**.

TURNED OUT **JUST** LIKE MY **MOTHER**.

MAYBE YOU'LL **UNDERSTAND** WHEN YOU HAVE **KIDS** OF YOUR OWN.

I DON'T WANT **KIDS**.

I **HATE** BEING A GIRL!

IT **HURTS**.

THEY DON'T CALL IT **THE CURSE** FOR NOTHING.

MAY, 1977

WAKE UP!

IT'S THAT **COMEDIAN** I WAS TELLING YOU ABOUT!

THEY DON'T KNOW WHAT TO DO WITH THEMSELVES NOWADAYS.

RIDICULOUS!

WELL, I'M A **RAMBLIN'** GUY...

HAHAHAHA!

I SHOULD GO TO BED.

OH, JUST WATCH THE **SHOW** WITH ME. AND MAKE US A COUPLE OF THOSE **FLUFFERNUTTERS** WHEN THE COMMERCIAL'S ON.

AND THE LATE **LATE** MOVIE IS **KILLDOZER**!

I'M AN OLD **COWHAND**... FROM THE **RIO GRANDE**!

CRAZY AS THE **BIRDS**!

143

JUNE, 1977

I THINK I'M GONNA BE AN **ARTIST** WHEN I GROW UP.

MY **MOM** THINKS I'D BE REALLY **GOOD** AT IT.

I **USED** TO WANT TO BE AN ARTIST.

WOAH, YOU'RE **SMOKING**?!

I JUST **SNUCK** ONE FROM DAD.

AREN'T YOU AFRAID OF GETTING **CAUGHT**?

YEAH. BUT...

I WON'T.

WHO'S D.V.?

DARTH VADER.

WHO'S **DARK INVADER**?

DARTH VADER! HAVEN'T YOU SEEN **STAR WARS** YET?

NOT YET.

144

HE'S THE **BAD GUY.**

I ALWAYS LIKE THE BAD GUY **BEST.**

ME TOO. I ALWAYS **FEEL SORRY** FOR THEM. I THINK THEY'RE USUALLY JUST **MISUNDERSTOOD.**

MY COUSIN SAYS EVERYTHING WILL **CHANGE** IN **GRADE SEVEN.**

MY BROTHER SAYS THAT, TOO.

MY BROTHER ALSO SAYS HIS **WANG GROWS** WHENEVER HE SEES WONDER WOMAN.

WHAT?

HIS **WANG.** IT **GROWS.**

EW.

FUCK, PEOPLE ARE **WEIRD.**

SO WHAT **DO** YOU WANT TO BE WHEN YOU **GROW UP,** ANYWAY?

A PSYCHIATRIST.

THANK YOU...

Michael Aronson, for your constant support, insight, and for preventing me from giving up.

RM Vaughan, for your invaluable help and advice.

Billy Mavreas, for giving me a push.

Everyone who cheered me on.

THE NIGHT WIND

BY EUGENE FIELD 1850–1895

Have you ever heard the wind go "Yooooo"?
T'is a pitiful sound to hear!
It seems to chill you through and through
With a strange and speechless fear.
T'is the voice of the night that broods outside
When folk should be asleep,
And many and many's the time I've cried
To the darkness brooding far and wide
Over the land and the deep:
Whom do you want, O lonely night,
That you wail the long hours through?"
And the night would say in its ghostly way:
"Yooooooooo! Yooooooooo! Yooooooooo!"

My mother told me long ago
(When I was a little tad)
That when the night went wailing so,
Somebody had been bad;
And then, when I was snug in bed,
Whither I had been sent,
With the blankets pulled up round my head,
I'd think of what my mother'd said,
And wonder what boy she meant!
And "Who's been bad to-day?" I'd ask
Of the wind that hoarsely blew,
And the voice would say in its meaningful way:
"Yooooooooo! Yooooooooo! Yooooooooo!"

That this was true I must allow –
You'll not believe it, though!
Yes, though I'm quite a model now,
I was not always so.
And if you doubt what things I say,
Suppose you make the test;
Suppose, when you've been bad some day
And up to bed are sent away
From mother and the rest –
Suppose you ask, "Who has been bad?"
And then you'll hear what's true;
For the wind will moan in its ruefulest tone:
"Yooooooooo! Yooooooooo! Yooooooooo!"

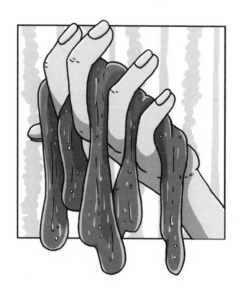

First-time author D. Boyd is a self-taught cartoonist originally from Saint John, New Brunswick. After many years in advertising, and later pursuing filmmaking, she moved to Montreal and reignited her love of illustrating, writing, and especially, comics.

Photo by Michael Aronson